LOVE

Christian Romance, Marriage, Friendship

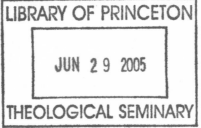
Diogenes Allen

© 1987 by Cowley Publications.

All rights reserved.

Published in the United States of America
by Caroline Press

International Standard Book Number 0-9653625-1-5

(Previously published by Cowley Publications,
ISBN 0-936384-47-6)

cover design by Charles H. Heffling

Caroline Press 133 Cedar Lane
Princeton, NJ
08540

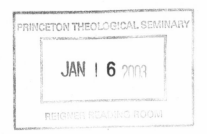

LOVE

BOOKS BY THE SAME AUTHOR

The Reasonableness of Faith

The Path of Perfect Love

The Traces of God in a Frequently Hostile World
    (accompanies video Significance of Suffering)

Three Outsiders: Pascal, Kierkegaard, and Simone Weil

Christian Belief in a Post Modern World

Quest: the Search for Meaning through Christ

Philosophy for Understanding Theology

Primary Reading in Philosophy for Understanding Theology
    (with Eric O. Springsted)

Nature, Spirit, and Community: Issues in the Thought of Simone Weil
    (with Eric O. Springsted)

Spiritual Theology: An Introduction to Yesterday's Christian Spiritually for Our Use Today
    (accompanies videos Eight Deadly Thoughts and What is Christian Spirituality)

Available from T.B.A., Princeton Theological Seminary, P.O. Box 821,
    Princeton, NJ 08542-0803. Tel. (609) 497-7735

Temptation

Available from Caroline Press
133 Cedar Lane, Princeton, NJ 08450

Also available: videos Significance of Suffering, Eight Deadly Thoughts, What is
Christian Spirituality, and Temptation with a study guide for Adult Education classes.
Write: Media Services, Princeton Theological Seminary,
P.O Box 821, Princeton, NJ 08542-0803

In gratitude to Jane M. Allen
who has had a hand in everything I have written.

Acknowledgments

This book was written during a sabbatical leave from Princeton Theological Seminary while I was a Fellow at the Center of Theological Inquiry, Princeton, New Jersey. It is my pleasure publicly to thank Thomas W. Gillespie, the President of the Seminary, and James I. McCord, the Chancellor of the Center, for their generous encouragement and support.

Table of Contents

Introduction

Whenever we hear the word "love" in our society, we immediately think of romance. Even though there are many other sorts of love, such as the love between parents and children, love between children, love between friends, love of country, love of nature, and even love of ideas, as well as love of music and the other fine arts, still it is romantic love between a man and a woman that usually comes to mind when we hear the word "love."

This has not always been true. The idea of romantic love is a creation of the Middle Ages. This does not mean that people before that did not fall in love, but it is relatively recent that people have prized romantic love between man and woman as an *ideal*, as something splendid, as something that ennobles people and enables them to realize their natures, as perhaps the highest and most desirable form of love. We are so used to this view of love that we find it hard to realize that it is radical. Yet prior to the Middle Ages, romantic passion was considered to be a misfortune. In classical times it was friendship that was praised as the highest form of love between human beings. That friendship is a very distant second to romantic love in our scale of values indicates how much our ideals have changed. There are literally thousands of books, not to mention magazine stories, films and soap operas, whose theme is romantic love. A story devoted solely to genuine friendship is hard to find. One of the few that comes to mind, *Three Comrades*, concerns three ex-servicemen who go into business together after the war. In order to express the nature and extent of their friendship, however, the author has to introduce the tragic romantic love of one of the comrades for a dying woman. That tragic love, rather than the devoted support of two of the comrades for their friend in his sorrow, becomes the focus of interest. Generally speaking, we simply do not find the ups and downs of friendship enough to sustain our interest in a story.

The notion of passionate yet ennobling love between a man and woman as a distinctive way to human fulfillment posed a new question for Christian thinkers when it first appeared in the twelfth century. More than one medieval writer sought to find a way to reconcile the two great commandments—that we are to love God and to love our neighbor—with romantic love, which is not a commandment at all. (St. Paul's injunctions that a husband is to love his wife is not an endorsement of romantic love). Denis de Rougemont in his classic work, *Love in the Western World*, goes so far as to claim that the exalted status of romantic love actually made it a rival *religion* to Christianity in some circles. This daring hypothesis has now been rejected by most scholars. In addition, Irving Singer, a philospher at M. I. T., who has just published the second volume of a highly regarded trilogy on love in western culture, distinguishes between romantic love and courtly love, the latter a literary creation of the troubadours in the High Middle Ages. Courtly love often involved a married woman and a suitor and its most important theme was the unattainability of the lady. This distinction is useful, and I myself shall be concerned with romantic in contrast to courtly love.

Even though Singer and others claim that de Rougemont went too far, nonetheless Singer himself champions a modified view of romantic love between man and woman. He pits it against the tendency of Christianity to turn us toward God and neighbor and away from romance as a source of self-realization. The love of God that comes from above is contrasted to human passionate love between man and woman, and it is to the potential of romantic love that Singer directs us. In their different ways such writers claim that there is a tension between Christian love and romance which requires our attention, whether we be Christians or not, given the importance each of them has in our society.

We can find, however, little guidance on the relation between divine love, which is frequently referred to as "agape," and human passionate love. Secular marriage manuals, advice on the mechanics of sexuality, and psychologically based studies of love and sex usually ignore Christianity or cast it in the form of a repressive social force. Most Christian people receive little instruction on what it is to love God and their neighbor that can equip them to deal with romantic love maturely. To most Christians, love of God means that we are to have a sense of gratitude for our existence and for the gift of forgiveness, and that we are obliged to obey Christian ethical teaching. We are taught that everyone is our neighbor and that we are to help all people as best we can. This in itself is fine, but it does not sufficiently equip people to come to terms with the passion of romantic love, especially with its accompanying notion that love between man and woman is the main place to find happiness.

I am not suggesting that in our love of God and love of neighbor our emotions ought to be of such an intensity that Christian agape can be a successful rival of romantic love for our allegiance. Rather I am claiming that there are in fact vital connections between the two great commandments of Christianity and the widespread belief in and desire for romantic love. People can be greatly helped in understanding their religion, as well as enriched in their practice of a passionate love of another by knowing those connections. One of the main purposes of this book is to show the vital connections between Christianity and the widespread ideal and experience (for they are not identical) of passionate love between man and woman. I will show how agape is an indispensable

Introduction

ingredient of love between a man and a woman, and on the other hand, how romantic love can make a vital contribution to our love of God and neighbor.

However much friendship has been made to play second to romantic love in modern western culture, it continues to exist as a significant form of love between people. Social and geographic mobility have made it an especially hard relationship to sustain over a long period of time, but it is such an important way in which human beings find life worth living that it deserves careful consideration in its own right. Like romantic love between a man and woman, friendship requires agape as an ingredient. Even though friendship and romantic love are very different, they have one thing in common: the need to love our neighbor as we love ourselves. If they lack that as an integral part, then both of them lack what they need to sustain themselves. They will fail to be proper realizations of themselves, and because of that failure can even become destructive. They can all too easily become, for example, dominated by possessiveness and jealousy.

Our situation today has become more complicated because of our sceptical reaction to the *ideology* of romantic love. Falling in love is indeed thrilling, but people have learned from experience that the thrill does not last and that people who fall in love do not live happily ever after. In addition, Freud's ideas on sex and love have been used as a rationalization for pursuing sexual pleasure that is free from all moral considerations, on the grounds that such inhibitions are simply the product of our socialization. For some people today it is regarded as a mark of maturity to be cynical about love and marriage, and to engage in sexual pleasure with as little emotional involvement and commitment as possible.

This kind of sensuality, defended in the name of "science," is not a new phenomenon. For example, Plato's dialogue *Phaedrus* opens with a long speech by a well-known Sophist—the ancient equivalent of an "up-to-date" and "well informed" person—in defense of sex without love or commitment. But we today are particularly vulnerable to modern sensuality and cynicism, not because Freudian popularizations are necessarily sound, but because our theory of romantic love is so unrealistic. If the ideal of romantic love is rejected, there is no viable reason generally available in our culture to resist sensuality. Then sexual practices become simply a pragmatic matter of personal tastes—whether heterosexual, homosexual, or bisexual—from the most casual and promiscuous to any number of arrangements people choose to make. The danger of disease, the threat of unwanted pregnancies, the inconvenience of abortion, and the like become the only consideration.

I myself am not ready to give up on love, and I think it can be distinguished from the unrealistic expectations which have surrounded it in recent centuries. In this respect I am in agreement with Irving Singer, perhaps the most philosophically profound defender of romantic love today, but his approach is a secular, perhaps even an anti- Christian, one. I myself will seek to free romantic love of its lack of realism, which has rightly made it subject to criticism, in a religious context. On the other hand, my view is idealistic. That is, I believe both friendship and romantic love are ideals to be striven for with varying degrees of success. Therefore in this book I will try to give an account of these two loves, as well as of marriage and Christian love in their highest forms, so that people in our society can have an accurate but unacademic knowledge of what they are, why they are worth striving for, and what it takes for them to be realized. The only defense against sensuality is the reality of these loves themselves. To describe them and their worth and cost accurately gives people a genuine choice of how they are to live.

Introduction

I shall begin, then, with the very familiar and biblical idea of the love of neighbor. However familiar it is as an idea, we are actually very unfamilar with it as a reality. Not only do we fail to practice it very well, we really do not understand it very well even as an idea. This is not because of any particular obtuseness on our part. It is because love of neighbor is a *perfect* love, and perfection is not common. Unless we have experienced perfect love, we are unlikely to have a very clear idea of what it is. I shall therefore give an example of the experience of perfect love so that what I am talking about will be quite concrete, before we consider in detail friendship, romantic love, and marriage.

Love consists not in feeling great things, but in having great detachment and in suffering for the beloved.

St. John of the Cross
Ascent of Mt. Carmel

The Experience of Perfect Love

My example of the experience of perfect love is based on Samuel Taylor Coleridge's famous poem, "The Rhyme of the Ancient Mariner." In that poem a strange old man stops a party of wedding guests. In spite of their protests, he insists that he must tell them a story as his penance for a crime he committed long ago when he was a sailor. He seems to cast a spell on one of the members of the party, who agrees to stay behind and hear the old mariner's confession.

What the mariner actually did was in itself trivial. It happened on a voyage to the south Atlantic, where the former good weather had turned to fog and ice, an ominous sign. However, spirits lifted when an albatross was spotted and hailed by the crew as a good omen: "As if it had been a Christian soul,/ We hailed it in God's name." The albatross continued to follow the ship and seemed to enjoy the company of the sailors. But the men took their good fortune for granted, even when the weather turned and the ship was guided to safety through the ice floes by the one bird which continued to accompany the ship. Then one day, the old mariner confesses to the wedding guest, in high spirits he pointlessly shot the innocent albatross. The other sailors, heedless of the cruelty of this thoughtless act, cheered his success; as a result of this senseless killing, however, the ship was becalmed. After many days of suffering, first from bitter cold and then from heat and the lack of water, the men became enraged with the mariner. They hung the dead albatross around his neck to single him out as the guilty party. The mariner now came to hate and curse the dead bird, to despise his miserable fate and his own stupidity.

Still the mariner's penance is not complete. As the days go by the ship is visited by the spectre of death, a ghostly ship, and the entire crew dies. The mariner is completely alone; he tries to pray, but his heart is "dry as dust." In his loneliness the mariner begins to watch the moon rising over the water and the creatures of the deep, their beauty and their happiness. It is then that a radical change occurs: "A spring of love gushed from my heart,/ And I blessed them unaware." This strange new vision means that the mariner is finally free to pray. At the same moment he is liberated from the albatross, the "cross" around his neck. He gazes at the water snakes moving around the ship and

> something welled up within him to which he could only
> give the name "love" and he *suddenly felt grateful for
> them*. Not because they were of any use to him, because
> they were not; and not necessarily because he *liked*
> them: he found them strangely beautiful but possibly
> not attractive. The experience was something quite dif-
> ferent from this—it was gratitude for their existence.[1]

The mariner had pointlessly killed the albatross. He had failed to recognize it as something which existed apart from his own interests. He had seen the bird only from his own selfish point of view. He had just seen it as something to shoot for the fun of it. The whole world existed as something with himself at its center; nothing else was recognized as a center of existence. His point of view was the only point of view.

But then suddenly he saw that the slimy things in the sea existed apart from himself. They had a life of their own apart from any use they could be to him, apart from whether they looked beautiful or repulsive to him. To escape for a moment from looking at everything from his own point of view—to let them be independent of himself—brought to him the experience of perfect love.

However strange this tale may be and however trivial the act of killing a bird may seem, Coleridge has shown us what enables us to have an experience of perfect love. Fundamental to the experience of perfect love is the loss of self-concern. It is to stop worrying about how useful things may be to us, and instead to pay attention to them as separate centers of reality. Usually we are aware only of ourselves as centers of reality and forget that each of us is but one reality among billions and billions of others. We experience others not as centers of value in themselves, but as beings in orbit around ourselves.

In the first chapter of Genesis, after the description of each act of creation it is written, "God saw that it was good." This phrase is repeated six times. It means, I take it, that it was "good" that the creatures were there—not because they were needed by God, nor because they were useful to him, nor because they were part of himself, nor even because he was their maker (although everything God makes is good). Rather, "God saw that it was good" means that he saw, recognized, and respected the creatures' presence simply because they were what they were. He recognized their reality. Even though they depended on him utterly, God let them be there as realities in their own right. God does not seek to be the only reality nor the only focus of interest. Rather, he creates other realities, other foci of interest and value.

But *we* do not see other creatures this way. Most of the time we do not recognize them as independent of ourselves. We see them only as they orbit around ourselves. Like the ancient mariner, in one way or another, we "kill" the reality of other things. We destroy it; we cover it over by allowing only ourselves to really matter. It is as though only we really exist.

One night I was putting one of my boys to bed. I was very pleased with the way I was looking after him and being considerate. Then suddenly he bit me, and I slapped him very hard. In an instant my concern for him had vanished, and I was reacting to the outside world solely and completely from my own point of view.

Most of our lives are spent that way. We do not experience ourselves as one reality among many, but we experience ourselves as a very special reality. Even when we feel lowly and unhappy, nothing matters as much as our own lowliness and unhappiness. Even people with very low self-esteem remain at the center of their own world and evaluate everything from their own perspective. If we could escape from the isolation of our own worlds, then perhaps we would be able to see the world as God sees it. He sees it as good; he sees it with perfect love.

When the ancient mariner suddenly felt grateful for the slimy things in the sea, even though they were of no particular use to him, the dead albatross fell from his neck of its own accord. The ship suddenly left the becalmed waters and was transported to safety. The mariner had found his redemption by finding his way out of a self-defined world into a world of other realities.

This sudden change is the result of a slow transformation. The forces which cause us to see everything from our own point of view are numerous and powerful. Perceiving others with perfect love is a distant goal which we may move toward, and occasionally we may be blessed with a momentary vision of the independent reality of things. The ancient mariner's suffering and his awareness that he suffers because of a callous deed, enables him to repent of what he has done. Only then does he temporarily escape from the tenacious hold of his ego. Yet it is enough for him to glimpse a truth about himself and to achieve a proper regard for other people—something he learned from an experience with a bird and some reptiles.

Once when visiting the director of a communications disorder clinic, I noticed a plaque on the wall with these words, "Love is the Otherness of Things." I was told that both children who have speech problems, as well as older people with impaired speech because of a stroke, must have a great desire to communicate. It is so difficult and takes so much persistent effort that unless people want to reach out to others and make themselves understood, they usually fail to overcome their handicap. They must love the "otherness" of things. They often begin to have this love because it is so painful to be cut off from others.

There is another aspect to perfect love, the aspect of compassion:

> To love a thing is to see a thing as existing in its own
> right—to go out to its existence. And to go out to a
> thing in this way when it is a living thing, and particu-
> larly when it is a living person, is *fundamentally to have
> pity for it*. . . For the insight into its existence is at the
> same time an insight into its suffering, its defenceless-
> ness, its profound vulnerability.[2]

To love perfectly is not simply to see that all else is independent of oneself and so ought to be loved as it is. Perfect love of a living thing is the recognition that it has an inside. To love it is to recognize what it is like to *be* that object. From the outside it looks gloriously radiant; inside, it is fragile and suffering.

Part of the reason we suffer is because we have a deep need of recognition. This is true of people of all ages, classes, races and circumstances. Each of us does have worth, genuine preciousness, but it is not properly recognized and external circumstances do not reflect it. For example, how often we hear of a factory or company having to lay off workers, or of a people who have no one to look after them. Think of how often we feel hurt and bruised going about our daily tasks. If someone loved us perfectly, our true worth would be recognized. Until someone does love us perfectly we will never experience or know for ourselves our own true worth.

All of us have a pressing, boundless desire to be loved properly. Ironically we all want so badly to be properly recognized that we ourselves are unable to recognize others. Each of us needs and desires more recognition than we are in turn able to give. What we need and seek is true community: community in which each of us is but one reality among many, paying proper attention to others and in turn receiving the affectionate attention of others.

Marriage and friendship are two such communities, or at least they can be. For them to become genuine communities, however, a balance between the need to be properly loved and the ability to recognize others must be achieved. Let me illustrate this first with friendship.

Once, while walking across the campus where I teach, I met a friend of mine coming out of one of the guest accommodations that is used for continuing education programs. We warmly greeted each other and I said to my friend, "Did you just get here?" He looked uncomfortable and began to explain that he had been here for nearly a week. Immediately I thought to myself: "You've been here nearly a week and not gotten in touch, even though I live only a few blocks away? Are you really as much a friend as I thought?" Then I stopped myself. My friend explained how tired he was from overwork and that he had come to stay at our center in order to read quietly and recuperate, but had spent most of the time sleeping because he had caught the flu. Before he had finished, I had stopped my negative thoughts; because I had realized that precisely because he was a friend, he was not obliged to look me up whenever he came to town. Our friendship should not prescribe his behavior. He ought to have the freedom to do exactly as he wishes with his time when he comes to the town in which I live. A friendship ought to be strong enough to bear the fact that friends do not always want to be with each other, and that this does not mean that they do not care for each other greatly. Happily I realized this in time to let my friend know that he did not owe me an apology at all, and that I was delighted to see him.

At the time I was indeed taking a risk. Maybe his behavior did indicate that he really was not my friend, or not as great a friend as I had thought. If I had taken offense and interpreted his behavior that way, it is quite possible that my behavior would have soured our relation and might even have spelled the beginning of the end of our young friendship. As it turned out, I was just able to recognize his "otherness" by controlling my need to be recognized and respected by another human being, and not to feel as though I had been abused by his behavior. It was fortunate because I have since learned from his subsequent behavior that at that time he was indeed a friend who cared for me. I have learned, too, over the years that he is a person who needs a great deal of solitude. His work places great emotional demands on him and from time to time he needs to be alone. I had run into him on one of those occasions, not knowing about this aspect of his personality.

Every friendship has its own peculiarities. Different kinds of behavior mean different things in each friendship. In this case, my friend's failure to get in touch when it would have been easy to do so did not mean what it usually does. However much friendships differ, they all must have as an ingredient respect for the freedom, independence, reality, or "otherness" of the friend. Otherwise the friendship will be marred by possessiveness and restrictions on individuality. In order for a friendship to prosper and be sustained, a love that is the recognition of "otherness" must be present. There are other ways that friendships fail, as we shall see later when we discuss friendship in detail, but a balance between our need to be properly recognized and recognition of the independence of another person must always be present.

The same is true of romantic love. One of the most widely held convictions about romantic love is that it usually does not last. People fall passionately in love; often they get married; then after a while, the intensity of the passion fades. It may even die altogether. One of the sad things about romantic love, we feel, is that it cannot be sustained indefinitely, or even for a particularly long time, and that is one of the reasons many people think that the idea of life-long commitment is irrational. Marriage in our culture is based on romantic love, yet it is also widely held in our culture that romantic love cannot be sustained. Since it is assumed that we can only be happy with the person we love, marriage and romantic love have often been seen as incompatible states. Marriage has even been regarded as the enemy of romantic love, turning the wonderful spontaneity of romance into the mundane, humdrum business of daily life. From this point of view, lifelong marriage is often seen to be cruel; it commits people to a lifelong relation after the joy of love is gone, and prevents the possibility of life with another person who can reawaken love in us.

Kierkegaard, writing in the middle of the nineteenth century, was very aware of this alleged conflict. In an essay we shall examine in detail in the next chapter, he argues that marriage actually enhances romantic love, instead of curtailing it. He argues that the ethical commitment to another person in marriage is precisely what enables the spontaneity of romantic love to achieve the stability and longevity that it is unable to provide by itself. It is precisely our recognition of "otherness," which is properly honored by a commitment, that enables us to achieve what romantic love seeks but by itself cannot attain—namely, to love another person always.

At this point we can indicate one way in which the recognition of "otherness" helps sustain romantic love. When we are in love, we seek to be united with the person we love. Usually we think in terms of sexual union. This is indeed part of what union means, but it also means being united in other aspects of our lives. How is such union to be understood? The question is relevant to all forms of love, not only romantic love. To love is to reach out, to move from isolation to involvement with another person. We have already indicated in the case of friendship something of the nature of that involvement: we are not to fill another person's life completely. On the contrary, friendship requires a profound respect for each other's independence, which includes the freedom to lead much of life apart from one another.

Romantic love, which for us in modern western society provides the basis of marriage, calls for a much more extensive involvement with another person than friendship does, and not merely because it involves sexual intimacy and child-rearing as well as legal obligations. Some philosophers and poets have regarded the union of romantic love to be a mutual absorption, so that two people become one person. Even though not literally possible, this unrealistic goal affects people's attitudes and behavior, often causing them to leave little space for independent thought and action as they vainly seek to achieve such a union.

The union or oneness that Christianity endorses in romantic love and marriage is that of a common or *shared life*. Two people in marriage remain distinct individuals. They are not to try to become one by absorbing each other, but to respect the irreducible "otherness" of each person in their love. Without that respect, romantic love becomes possessive. It does not allow each person to be a person in his or her own right. The union of romantic love that issues in marriage is to be symbolized not by a circle, which has only one center, but by an ellipse, which has two foci. When the two points of an ellipse come closer and closer together, the figure constructed around them becomes more and more nearly circular; when the two points coincide, so that there is only one, the figure becomes a circle. An ellipse is thus an excellent geometric figure to symbolize the common life **two** distinct people create together and share. Each person has some thoughts and actions apart from the other, but each shares in the other's thoughts and actions by his or her interest, support, and commitment. This involvement creates a common or shared life. Such a shared life does not belong to either person singly, and it cannot be divided neatly into parts each belonging exclusively to one person. Rather, it is a life that has an existence only to the extent that two people passionately love each other and commit themselves to each other, while at the same time each recognizes the irreducible distinctiveness of the other. Romantic love can achieve this unique and delicate relation in marriage only if each person can recognize, respect, and cherish the independent reality of the other.

There is another way that people try to deal with the tensions and problems that arise in living together, and it is closely connected to this attempt to achieve union by absorbing one another. They struggle to increase the intensity of the passion felt in romantic love, assuming that the passion of romantic love itself can overcome all difficulties. When difficulties do not go away, then accusations arise; one does not love the other enough; the proof of an insufficient love is the existence of the unresolved difficulties. Yet to expect the intensification of an emotion to deal with the tensions that arise out of the fact that each of us is a distinct individual is actually to pressure a person to surrender his or her individuality. Romantic love needs to be combined with another kind of love in order to deal with the difficulties of life together at close quarters. Sheer intensity of passion cannot overcome the strains because the attempt to achieve complete absorption in one another is destructive to each genuine and legitimate reality.

The recognition of "otherness," then, must be integrated with friendship and romantic love. It takes very little effort on our part initially to be attracted to another person either in a friendly way or romantically, but it takes a considerable effort to achieve and sustain our recognition of the irreducibility of that person's reality. The independent reality of another may suddenly and unexpectedly strike us, as it did the ancient mariner, but such spontaneous moments are not enough. The proper and natural recognition of other realities must become part of our character. The need to be properly recognized and loved by others is so great that, without considerable effort and cultivation, we are unable to restrain that need and our many other needs sufficiently to realise that other people are not merely in orbit around us. Other people attract us spontaneously because of our conscious and unconscious needs; nevertheless the restraint of those needs is not a spontaneous matter. Unless we do restrain our needs sufficiently, however, other people never achieve that independence which is necessary for friendship to prosper and romantic love to be sustained. This restraint is not a religious option that we may or may not choose without any consequences. The recognition of the reality of others is not only a Christian duty, but a necessary ingredient in those wonderful human loves, friendship and romance.

This ingredient is often present in people's friendships and romantic love without their realizing it. They quite naturally assume that their friendship and love for one another has no religious ingredient, but it is this ingredient that enables friendship and romantic love to be properly themselves, and not sour or fade. The recognition of "otherness" is an act which *disregards* people's personal traits. We recognize "otherness" by the shared characteristic people have, namely their existence as distinct realities. Friendship and romantic love, in contrast to this, are directed to the *specific* personality of each person—to whatever makes us different from one another. It is the distinctive person that is loved in friendship and romantic love, not the feature which everyone has in common.

This contrast has frequently been described as the difference between a love which is impartial, making no distinction and given to all, and all human loves which are partial and for particular people only. This is evident in the parable of the Good Samaritan, which Jesus told in response to a Pharisee's question, "But who is my neighbor?" (Lk 10:29) A man on the road to Jericho is attacked by thieves and left by the side of the road, naked and badly beaten. Later, both a Levite and a priest walk past the stricken man without attempting to help him. Still later a Samaritan coming along the road stops and helps the man. He binds his wounds, and puts him on his animal and takes him to an inn. He leaves him in charge of the innkeeper, and promises to pay the innkeeper for any additional expenses when he passes on his return journey. The Samaritan stepped across the chasm between his sect and other Jews to help someone simply because he was a person in need. He does not do so because he finds the injured person attractive, or because he likes him, anymore than the mariner liked or was attracted by the slimy things in the sea. Such an impulse is very different from friendship and romantic love which are aroused by the attractiveness of another person, and may be very much affected by prejudice and the like. But in any case they are always partial, a love for a particular person and not for all people. They are not loves universally bestowed on any person simply in so far as he or she is a person.

Love of neighbor is the recognition of the *absolute* value of every person. Most of the time we are aware of the *relative* value of people. Relative value is determined by comparing people to each other in terms of their possessions, accomplishments, talents, looks, charm, and the like. Some people are more important than others in terms of their relative value, and we usually take more notice of people who rank higher than others on the scale of relative value. The man who had been robbed and beaten no longer had any possessions or clothing to indicate his social status, his relative value. Therefore the Good Samaritan must have recognized his absolute value.

It is a conviction of western society that every person has absolute value, or absolute significance. Yet in his excellent study *Morality: Religious and Secular,*[3] Basil Mitchell argues that this part of traditional morality is in danger of being abandoned today. It has been an objective of secular thinkers since the eighteenth century to replace religion with reason as the basis of ethics and society. It was thought that our traditional moral convictions, especially the absolute value of people, could be established by reason and did not need a religious basis. Mitchell and others claim that every philosophic attempt to find a basis for this moral conviction has failed. They argue that the only value people have which we can specify apart from a religious base is relative value, conditional value, limited value, which is determined by comparing people to each other or to other creatures.

Christianity is the source of the conviction that every person has an absolute value; it is not present in any philosophy prior to the advent of Christianity. Stoicism came closest to it, claiming that all people have dignity because they have a *logos* or reason, but this

20

still left out the retarded, mentally ill, or senile. This conviction is not to be found in any other religion: Hinduism, Buddhism, Islam, or even Judaism. Only in Christianity is it made absolutely clear that all of us have absolute value or significance. Christians do not always live up to this conviction in practice, but they certainly recognize criticisms of failure to live up to it. It is their avowed aim.

According to Christianity our absolute value is based on God. Only God is wholly good, utterly and wholly pure, utterly and wholly free of defilement and corruption, and so only he has absolute value *in himself.* We have absolute value because we have been made by God to receive him; we are made to receive his presence. Without that as our destiny, we do not have absolute value.

The reality of an absolute good for which we are made is above the power of human intellect to establish. The intellect is the instrument we use for earthly concerns. An absolute good that gives us our absolute value is above the intellect because the intellect cannot give us certainty. Yet we do have certainty in the matter of our absolute value. It is present in our very bones; in our cry of anguish; in our untaught conviction that we have been made for more than wretchedness. Only those who recognize in their own hearts the anguish of what it is to be a human being, can act as the Good Samaritan acted. They can recognize that it is an outrage to allow a broken person to lie unnoticed and unattended.

Ernest Bevin, who led a dockworkers union in Britain in the twenties and thirties, stressed that the most important goal of the labor movement was for the workers to gain a sense of human dignity and to stop feeling like second class people. In the thirties a Parliamentary Commission was appointed to hear the case of the dockworkers. The management was represented by an eminent King's Counsel (a title of accomplishment in the legal profession). The dockers chose Ernest Bevin to put their case, even though he had little formal education and no legal or economic training. Bevin mastered the immensely complicated economic and legal facts relevant to the inquiry in a short time and presented the docker's case magnificently. He became known as the " Docker's K.C." and it was a point of pride among the dockers that one of their own was able to make their case.

We have learned from Arthur Miller's play how humiliating it can be to be a salesman. But it is also true that people in positions of prestige often have to endure humiliations daily in order to maintain their position in a firm. One of the reasons many students, teachers, and professors are so discouraged is because the meaning of what we do in our schools and universities has changed. The meaning of learning—the liberation of the mind and soul, access to vital truth, the creation of a better person—is now so remote from actual practice that it has become necessary to plead for it. Without such goals in our educational practices, we actually degrade people.

Absolute value can be recognized in our own persons through our response to the pain of humiliation or degradation. It can also be discovered in a much more positive way through humility. Humility is utterly different from humiliation. Humility does not lower us. Being humble is not to denigrate our actual talents and achievements, nor to lie about ourselves. It is rather to recognize the truth that our possessions, talents, and accomplishments do not raise us above others. They simply move us further along the horizontal plane of life so that we are ahead of some and behind others. Being ahead does not raise us over anyone; nor does being behind lower us. Humility is the recognition that however much we have acquired or achieved we are essentially like others: creatures of the earth. Nothing we do or have that distinguishes us from other people can change that status. Humility is to recognize this truth and to have it become part of the substance of our character and outlook so that it affects every thought, perception and action. Humility does not lower us, but allows us to be elevated; it enables us to recognize the absolute value conferred on us by God's invitation to share his life. Humility is felt to be deflating only to the extent to which our self-understanding is determined for us by our relative place along the horizontal continuum of life. Perhaps this is why Dag Hammerskjold recorded this remark in his notebook *Markings*, "To be humble is *not to make comparisons*." (He was also aware of the nature of perfect love. "To have humility is to experience reality, not *in relation to ourselves*, but in its sacred independence.")[4]

Part of the task of life, according to the Christian vision, is to learn how to live with each other as people who have both absolute and relative value. We are not above or below each other, but we do differ from each other. Some of the relative differences are spurious; they signify no genuine value and part of the task of life is to free ourselves from their power over us. Yet some of the differences are real; for example, strength, knowledge, and the ability to create are truly valuable.

Friendship and romantic love are two of the most important spheres where we learn to deal with each other as people with both absolute and relative value. It is in these common and daily aspects of life that we learn to combine our attraction to what distinguishes people from each other and causes us to value or care profoundly for a particular person with the absolute value that every person has. In friendship and romantic love we need to recognize the absolute value of another person in his or her "otherness," a recognition which is necessary for both friendship and romantic love to prosper. We can of course become so interested in the people we particularly love that we fail to recognize that other people besides our friends and lovers have absolute value as well. We may so favor those we love over others that we even act unjustly. Nonetheless, both friendship and romance are relationships where we can grow in our awareness of absolute value; such an awareness is necessary for friendship and romance to prosper. We may in these relationships begin to actualize the love of our neighbors.

Anders Nygren, a Swedish theologian, sparked off a major debate that lasted over three decades with his influential book *Agape and Eros*, first published in 1932. He not only *contrasts* Christian love (agape) and human love (eros), as I have, but also characterizes them in such a way that it is impossible for the two to be combined. According to Nygren, Christian love (agape) is the love of God which comes down to us and is utterly unrelated to all love which arises out of our own nature (eros). God's love is utterly unmotivated by any worth in the objects of his love; rather, his love creates value in what otherwise has no value. We are unable to love God; any love that springs from our nature is motivated by the value or worth of the object, and it seeks to acquire or to possess the object. Thus all human love is selfish. We are, however, able to love our neighbors because we receive God's love and it flows through us to others.

I agree that agape refers in the first instance to God's love, and that the love of neighbor which we can exhibit has its source in God, whether we realize it or not. It is also true that agape, because it is impartially shown by God to the whole of creation, is not contingent on any value or worth in us. Nygren's characterization of agape as unmotivated by any value or worth in people, however, should not be interpreted to mean that Christian love denies our worth. God's saving grace, or his redeeming love of sinners, is indeed not given because we are worthy of it. Such love is indeed independent of any characteristics or worth we have. This does not mean we have no worth at all; we are still violated when we are injured by others, and something of value is still lost when people perish. Christianity clearly teaches that what God created is good and hence of worth and value, even though human beings have fallen from their initial created state. This is clear from the fact that we can recognize the value of non-human creatures, as did the mariner in Coleridge's poem. We too, in so far as we are realities, have value as well. It is precisely that value which we are commanded to recognize in loving the "otherness" of things. It is thus correct to say that love of neighbor, unlike friendship and romantic love, is not motivated by the particular features which distinguish people from each other. When we love our neighbor, we recognize a creature which has worth in so far as a person is a reality and is to be respected as one, and not reduced to an object orbiting around our interests, needs, wants, prejudices, and conveniences. People's reality and absolute value preclude such treatment.

Nygren argues that since all human loves (in contrast to agape) are motivated by the value of the object, they are not only partial—directed only toward those people and things which someone finds valuable—but also selfish. We love because we seek to gain satisfaction, reward, and fullfillment from what is loved. Only agape is unconcerned with any expectation of return. To love unselfishly, then, is to give and only to give. But this kind of loving is hardly compatible with friendship or romantic love. Friendship by its very nature does not exist unless the love is mutual, and one desires very much to enjoy the other person's company. Passionate love is a frustrated love unless it is returned. In either case one can hardly *not* desire to receive the love of another. Furthermore, to characterize agape as a love that only gives out, and hence to regard as selfish all our desires to receive love, is an attitude that leads people to despair of ever being able to love God and their neighbor. On the contrary, we indeed receive a great deal when we love God, and we hope to receive the love of our neighbor.

The Experience of Perfect Love

Where this attitude has gone wrong is its assumption that to receive or even to want to receive is of itself selfish. It is true that God is self-sufficient and does not lack anything. He loves us completely free of the distortions caused by the need to acquire. But our love is not necessarily selfish; we need to have friends and we are made in such a way that romantic love is greatly to be desired. Our problem is that all our needs, including our need to be recognized properly by others, are so powerful that they cause us to put others into orbit around ourselves. Egocentrism is indeed very powerful and encompasses most of our conscious and unconscious thoughts and actions; it is what causes us to *take* from others and not to *receive*. To receive we must recognize the reality of others and to perceive them free of the distortions caused by our needs.

Just as God when he created the universe pulled himself back, so to speak, in order to let other things exist besides himself, so are we to restrict ourselves in order to recognize the reality of others. The ingredient of respect for "otherness" enables us to *receive* the love of others in friendship and romantic love, to be free of selfishness. To receive from another requires profound respect. In fact, it takes exactly the same kind of respect to receive as it does to give. Unless another human being is respected as a reality independent of oneself, the act of giving becomes patronizing and insulting. Agape is not to be characterized as always giving and never receiving, or as freedom from even the desire to receive. Rather, agape is the profound respect for the reality of others, a respect which makes it compatible both with giving *and* receiving. When agape is present as an ingredient in friendship and romantic love, these relations in which we give and receive can be unselfish.

If we insist that the object of perfect love has no worth at all, in order to insure that we are loving unselfishly, then perfect love of what does have worth is impossible. The Son of God could not love the Father perfectly, nor the Father love the Son perfectly. Perfect love is the recognition of the worth of another free from the distortion of relative value and the distortions caused by our needs. That we find joy in loving, and not only give but receive does not render our love imperfect.

The fear that receiving is selfish led to self-defeating attempts in medieval spirituality and theology to Bonaventure's allegory of a "ladder of love." Aided by devotional practices, the soul was to ascend through several levels of love and become less and less concerned with desiring love for itself, until it reaches the level of perfection, which was to be utterly indifferent to receiving it. Luther's own experience with trying to practice this spirituality led him to despair of ever loving God. The fear that receiving love is selfish lies behind the Calvinist's question, "Are you willing to be damned for the glory of God?". That fear also lies behind Nygren's perverse claim that we are not commanded to love God, but to have faith only, and this in spite of the fact that Jesus said that the first and greatest of all the commandments is to love God. The same anxiety also leads Simone Weil occasionally to confuse the spiritual life with self-destruction. Iris Murdoch, the contemporary philosopher and novelist, fears that the expectation of any reward is inimical to genuine morality and love. She therefore says that we are to seek to be perfect "for nothing," and to reject belief in a personal God because it so powerfully encourages us to expect and seek rewards. All of these views can be very helpful in making us aware of the incredible power and tenacity of egotism, and indeed of our inability in this world to be free of it completely. But they do not show that to receive love is incompatible with perfect love.

But how does the love of God enter us so that we can show agape towards others? Dante, who has enriched us with his great poem *The Divine Comedy*, tells us that in his youth he met a girl at a party and was absolutely dumbstruck. Her beauty seemed to radiate perfection. Some years later as a young man he saw her walking down the street and had the same experience. He tells us that he was so completely full of love that if anyone had injured him he could not help but forgive him or her. This euphoria of love gradually faded away within a few days.

There is nothing particularly special about Dante's experience; it is to fall in love romantically. But Dante did something unusual with this experience. For him, the experience showed him the goal of his life: to seek to remain always the way he had been for the short time when inspired by Beatrice's beauty. Dante was to seek to be so filled with love that he would always be able to love his neighbor. What had been easy and joyous for a few days introduced him to his task: to love his neighbor always. Romantic love is not the same as love of neighbor. But the experience of romantic love introduced Dante to something that had a similarity to perfect love, and he made the decision to seek that perfect love whose likness he had experienced.

All of us have had moments, like Dante, when falling in love, we seem to float on air. The whole world seems wonderful, and we take in our stride people who normally irritate us and things that normally frustrate us. It is easy to be attentive and considerate with the beloved. These moments can also happen when we experience great beauty. For a while we are at peace and are elevated beyond our normal state, able to see human beings in a way that seems clearer to us and to see them more sympathetically. A particular person's idiosyncracies, which normally rub us the wrong way, no longer affect us adversely. For a while, we simply seem to be able to love anyone—to love our neighbor—without any effort at all.

These momentary occasions can be simply that. But they can also give us a glimpse of what it would be to love our neighbor all the time. To that extent such moments can be like little seeds, which if planted and nurtured, can grow and affect our character. We can become less and less dominated by the need to be recognized by others and more able to pay proper attention to others. The cultivation of those moments, however, does not happen automatically. We must deliberately make it our goal, taking the time and effort to meditate or to turn over in our minds these good experiences and to juxtapose them with other experiences—such as the memory of the time we were unfairly angry with a person's question. Such self-examination, if it has the purpose and goal of treating people with the respect every person ought to have as a neighbor, weakens the power of our egocentricity. Our character is strengthened so that the needs that dominate us and lead us to put others in orbit around us are more and more under our control. We become better and better at recognizing the independent reality of others and treating them accordingly.

Yet we do not become capable of loving others perfectly all at once. It is rather a goal that we aim for, a distant, and in this life, never attainable goal. But it is only because we have it as our goal that we improve. Momentary glimpses of perfect love motivate us, set us our task, make us realize that there is such a thing as perfect love, and that nothing less than perfect love will do. Anything less is a violation of a person, a violation of someone who has absolute value. By examining our thoughts, actions and feelings against the standard of love of neighbor, the small seeds of such a love are cultivated and nourished, so that our love of others improves with the improvement of our character.

The seeds of love can be planted very early. One woman shared with me what is no doubt a common experience, but one in which she recognized the beginnings of a love for others. As she grew older, she deliberately chose it to be her goal. She wrote to me about an experience of early childhood:

> During my pre-school years, I spent many evenings in the back of a dark church. I sat on my father's lap, wrapped safe in his arms. Together in the darkness we listened to the strong and sensitive voice of my mother read the words of the Advent story. "And in those days a decree went out from Caesar Augustus. . ."
>
> I sometimes cry even now as I recall the intensity of the sheer holiness of those nights wrapped within my father's warm love. . . . Those loves held me so tightly that I had no sense of myself. They were all human family loves, but a higher love made itself known to me. God's presence sought and found a little girl. He reached me through the channels of natural loves, so that they were something more than natural loves. I cannot of course dissect those loves and say that so much of it was human and so much of it was divine. Yet there was something unique in those moments and to this day when I give my allegiance to the love Christ calls on us to show I draw on those moments as the perfect love we are to have for others.[5]

It is not just in moments of beauty and warmth that God's love finds its way into us, but also through traumatic experiences of death, illness, and rejection. Each trauma can lead us into a reevaluation of what we are seeking in life. A close contact with death can clean and order one's emotional house. For a while pettiness and duplicity vanish, and a strong yearning for simplicity, integrity, and decency dominate. We can see ourselves with greater clarity and others more justly as the confusion and fog caused by our egocentricity abates for a time. As the trauma subsides, perhaps through the grace of forgetfulness, so does the clarity of one's heart. The experience and momentary realignment do not have much permanent effect on our character.

It is here that trauma, and the insight that art gives, and the value of religious ritual can meet and have a permanent effect on one's character. We could hardly tolerate art that constantly reopened us to half forgotten and half healed traumas; we could not stand to relive them fully. But an art that can reawaken the insight and feelings that *accompanied* a trauma would have moral efficacy. We could reexperience that release from pettiness and duplicity and vanity. Religious ritual, such as the celebration of the Lord's Supper, is like a work of art that portrays a trauma. That ritual is too rich to explore here, but this much we can say: Christ commanded us to recall his last meal with his disciples as a memorial to his sacrifical death. We could hardly tolerate a repetition of his crucifixion, or endure witnessing one. As a work of art recalls for us a trauma without fully reopening us to its almost unbearable impact, so too the ritual act of recalling Christ's crufixion and celebrating his love cleanses our lives and moves us along our course of becoming people who can love our neighbors.[6]

Simone Weil claims that school studies also have a potential religious value. For a ritual to nurture our love for others, we must have the power of paying attention to it properly; otherwise we let it come second to ourselves and our interests, thus greatly limiting its efficacy in moving us off center and closer to a proper regard for people. School studies improve our ability to pay attention to what is not ourselves. For to get a problem right in mathematics requires us to suspend for the moment our likes and dislikes, our wishes and our wants, in short, to empty ourselves. In the space that is created by our self-emptying, the problem we are solving can be perceived and understood more as it is in and of itself, free of the distortions of our personality. The frequent practice of attention to what is not ourselves in our school studies can become a part of our character. We can then consciously and deliberately make the effort to attend to other things, including art and religious ritual and prayer. We can become better and better at bringing ourselves to focus on something that is not ourselves, and gain some freedom from the needs which drive us to subordinate their reality to our own because we perceive them only in relation to ourselves. However the power of attention we can develop in academic studies does not automatically serve the purpose of moving us off center. The training in attention that school studies give us must be deliberately put to a moral and religious use by cultivation of those moments of insight that come to us. We can reflect on such things as the glorious experience of romantic love, or the utter joy of well-being we may have experienced as a child in our mother's or father's arms. We can allow art and religious ritual to reawaken the clarity that traumatic experiences give us.

Simone Weil recommends prayer in particular as having the power to lessen those forces that possess us and enfeeble our power to love others properly. She teaches us to pray the Lord's Prayer by attending solely to the words themselves, rather than to our thoughts about them. She claims that we will find ourselves powerfully elevated by love. It is very difficult to pray the Lord's Prayer with all your attention focused this way, as you can discover for yourself. However if you do, you will find that evil and unworthy feelings and thoughts you have towards others, as well as feelings of self-pity, gradually disappear. Were the sources of our evil and the sources of our egocentrism not still operative we would actually achieve perfect love permanently. As it is, our partial success indicates how very powerful the forces are that hold us in bondage and keep us from attending to the absolute value of people and the goodness of God's creation. But we are not powerless. We can make use of those moments when we are temporarily free to recognize that there is perfect love, and choose to become always what we are for a moment. We can cultivate the seeds of perfect love that come to us, and find ourselves able to love our neighbor, our friend, and our beloved more and more fruitfully.

We have now laid the foundations for a detailed examination of friendship and romantic love from a religious perspective. So far we have indicated that recognition of the independent reality of others—a large part of what is meant by Christian love—is a necessary ingredient in both friendship and romantic love. Yet there are other factors in both friendship and romantic love besides this religious ingredient. These human factors must be examined if we are to learn more about what enhances and what inhibits friendship and romantic love. From a Christian point of view, we are still within God's domain in making this examination because God has created us with the capacity for friendship and romance. Recognition of the "otherness of things," which God gives us, is an *uncreated* love because it is his own love at work in us. Friendship and romance are *created* loves; they arise from our human nature. This difference lies at the basis of the distinction between agape and our human loves, but this genuine difference must not blind us to the fact that our human loves are possible only because of our God-given capacities.

He removes the greatest ornament of friendship,
who takes away respect.

Cicero, *On Friendship*

Friendship

Our society is not organized in such a way as to promote long and deep friendships. We can see why this is so by contrasting ourselves to the ancient Greeks. The Greeks prized friendship highly, as can be seen from Aristotle's exaggerated but still revealing remark: "Friends live together."[7] It was possible for friends to spend a great deal of their daily life together, since freemen usually did not have to earn a living. They spent their time in the governing assembly and, since they formed the armed forces, training in the gymnasium. Friends frequently dined together and spent the evening in talk and entertainment. At least this was true of the men. Since they agreed by and large on what was valuable, as well as on the kind of citizen a person ought to be, the Greeks deliberately sought to promote those activities and institutions which would enable them to lead the particular kind of life they admired and enjoyed. It is this agreement which created a bond between citizens, and that bond was the basis of friendship. Friendship was much more a social-political relationship than in our society, where it is very much a private and personal matter.

Yet it is precisely this lack of integration into the political and economic structure of our society that makes friendship attractive to us. It is in friendship that we can detach ourselves to an extent from society's constraints. Friendship is rather like play; it does not connect directly with earning our living and pursuing social or political goals. In addition, unlike kinship, it is a purely voluntary relation. We are to a large extent free to choose our friends. Friendship is also unhampered by the emotional pressures of romantic love, which can sometimes make us feel a loss of control over our life and destiny, as well as free of the legally sanctioned obligations of marriage. Even though friendship is in some respects like play, it is a serious (but not somber) activity. It can matter enormously to our well-being. The fact that to enjoy friendship we must go against the flow of our political and economic life means that, for the sake of friendship, we must make a conscious effort.

Friendship requires us to develop our character. As we have already seen, respect for the independence of another is a necessary element of friendship, but this is only one of several elements which must be attended to for a friendship to develop and prosper. The same elements are present in romantic love and marriage as well. We shall, however, explore them in connection with friendship first because friendship is a much less complex relation; for example, it does not involve the possibility of rearing and nurturing children. Once we have become familiar with the ways friendship can prosper or fail, we can draw on a knowledge of these dynamics when we turn to romantic love and marriage and be free to treat matters which pertain only to them.

What is it that makes friendship a specific kind of love? Romantic love has a sexual element as an essential ingredient; friendship does not. Friendship can be fully itself without any sexual involvement. Sexual activity may occur in friendship, but it is an "accident," as Aristotle would say. That is, it is not necessary for it to be present in order for friendship to be friendship. Friendship is a very "unphysical" love.[8] Should friends express affection sexually, whether they are heterosexual or homosexual, the relation changes and begins to take on the characteristics of romantic love. For example, jealousy toward a third party, which is not nearly as common in friendship, is very common in romantic love and between "friend-lovers." The transition from friends to "friend-lovers" may also cause anxiety because the stakes have changed.[9]

Friendship

What is it that creates the bond of friendship? It usually arises because people have common interests and pursue common activities. They enjoy hearing each other's views and opinions about these pursuits, whether it be travel, literature, politics, movies, or baseball. Through these interests and activities friends reveal themselves in ways that distinguish them from others. It is sheer delight to move from isolation and impersonal relations to involvement with another person, to be valued and prized for what you have to say and can do by someone whose attitude matters to you. That such a person should find you of interest is gratifying. You are liked, respected, and attended to by someone you admire, with achievements in those areas that you yourself care about. It is enormously uplifting to be thus singled out, and you respond by showing similar liking, respect, and attention. This may be the beginning of friendship.

The bond of friendship is sheer delight at its inception. For a friendship to grow, develop and prosper, however, it must negotiate several obstacles. As people who are becoming friends get to know each other better, more of their personalities emerge. Two friends, though alike in the ways that cause the initial attraction, turn out to be different in other ways. Their points of view on public events, on day-to-day matters, on any and everything, are part of what they have to share with each other. A friendship may grow and develop if each person has a great deal to share, but if people are very unequal in what they have to offer, the friendship may soon be arrested in its development. Friendship is a relation of equality, or near equality. For example, two people of very unequal education may be attracted to each other by a common interest in baseball. They will soon find that although they can enjoy talking for a long time about baseball, there is little else they can talk about. Apart from baseball, what each has to offer is of little interest to the other. The friendship is genuine as far as it goes, but it does not go very far.

If you think this is snobbish, just think of those people whom you consider friends yet with whom you talk about only a very few things. Although you like and respect them, and enjoy dealing with them, your conversation tends to be in the same set phrases. Or simply notice how many of your close friends are very much like you in education and attainments.

Love of neighbor does not require the kind of equality in which each has something to give the other, nor does romantic love require basically equal attainments. We can love our neighbor without receiving anything in return, and people who fall in love can be of widely different levels of ability and achievement. But friendship is a mutual delight in what two personalities share. Since a friendship is a voluntary relation, it is perfectly all right for it to die out because of a lack of sufficient exchange. If the friendship has achieved a significant degree of development before reaching this limit, however, there may be regrets and embarassment when former friends meet, or even some resentment because one party feels rejected. But if we have developed a sense of the independent reality of other people, and recognize that friendship is essentially voluntary and that its dynamics require a near equality, these negative feelings can be dissipated. We can meet each other without embarassment or resentment.

On the other hand, the fact that friendship is a relation in which there is exchange also gives it a strength and durability. The exchange must be distinguished from what Aristotle called "a friendship of utility," a relation in which people do favors for each other on a *quid pro quo* basis.[10] They are "friends" in the sense that they can exchange favors, and each will do something for the other chiefly because each wants something in return. The "friendship" is tenuous because the people involved do not admire or esteem each other, or at any rate that is not the bond between them. It is rather that each has something the other wants, and so a mutually profitable exchange is possible. There is not necessarily anything evil in this, and it can even provide a form of association which can lead to friendship, but of itself it is not the sharing that is characteristic of friendship. Because the relation of friendship is based on mutual admiration of each other's personality, as exhibited in interests and accomplishments, friendship has the quasi-permanence of human personality. Once we are adults, we seldom change in fundamental ways, nor do we change quickly. So mutual attraction between those who are roughly equal in attainments has durability. Such people have a lot to offer each other as people, and so tend to remain friends.

If personality is the bond of friendship, it is also what can cause it to end. As people get to know each other better, they may discover things about each other which they do not like or approve. If a friendship is to grow, tolerance is necessary because very few people indeed are going to have the same taste in food, the same attitude toward drink, the same personal habits in dress, the same political convictions, the same religion, the same moral outlook. These are matters which none of us can avoid; sooner or later they will emerge in a friendship. They can of course be an opportunity for growth; one can come to like new foods, or to appreciate another religion. But intolerance or a low degree of tolerance, especially in a matter which means a great deal to another person, can damage a friendship and even cause it to end.

Here we see once again the importance of having developed a love for the "otherness of things." If we have learned to respect the independent reality of others, we can agree to differ on many matters. This will not save every friendship nor enable every friendship to continue to grow, but without some degree of the recognition of "otherness" every friendship will be hampered. Friendship is a wonderful place for tolerance and the recognition of "otherness" to grow and develop, precisely because we do care for another person.

This question of tolerance leads us to the dilemma of openness and concealment. There is a widespread assumption that in friendship you can reveal yourself to another person completely and without fear, because as a friend he or she accepts you as you are. At least this is an attitude that I frequently find in papers that my students write. It goes along nicely with our present cultural assumption that concealment is a sign of weakness, and that for two people to become completely transparent to each other is healthy. But this does not cohere with the results of empirical studies of friendship.[11] Of course people must reveal themselves to a degree for friendship to develop. Personal matters must be shared, and some evaluation of what is shared is unavoidable. But indiscriminate self-disclosure in friendship is not common. It takes time for people to show that they are trustworthy and will not pass on the intimate confidences of their friends. Friends therefore usually limit what they disclose to each other, and only gradually expose themselves as they gain confidence from each other's restraint, sensitivity, and trustworthiness. To reveal oneself to another person before that person has shown that he or she is worthy of such confidences indicates a lack of self-respect. It is almost as though one were to say: "Here I am, all of me. There is no need for you to take the trouble of being patient and showing by your tact and discretion your concern for me, because I am not worth all that effort." Likewise, a person who insists on "instant intimacy" at any price is a person who lacks respect for another person. The revealing of oneself which is built into the very nature of friendship requires its opposite, discretion and a degree of concealment. As friendship develops, people who care about each other do reveal and must reveal more and more of themselves. But effort and skill must still be exercised in dealing with areas that are particularly vulnerable.

Friendship, however, cannot thrive without some degree of candor and honesty. We cannot respond to what we learn about another with approval all the time. Besides, sometimes we want to know what a friend really thinks of our attitudes and behavior, even if it hurts. Do I dress appropriately? Do I talk too much? Am I too aggressive? Do I drink too much? A delicate balance between giving reassurance and being candid is required by friendship. Too much restraint, and the friends find themselves in a false relation, one lacking in honesty. Yet too much candor can cause so much pain that the genuiness of another's benevolence becomes suspect. The degree to which people can face certain truths about themselves, and the degree of skill and amount of affection people have for each other when they speak with candor, greatly determines the extent to which a friendship can develop, deepen, and endure.

It is very easy for people with the best will in the world to be at cross purposes. Suppose that we reveal something to our friend that we are ashamed of, hoping for sympathy and restraint? What if the friend believes that what is wanted is a frank response, and by making a frank response he or she inadvertently increases our sense of shame unbearably? This misunderstanding could lead to a severe set back in this friendship, and indeed might even prevent it from ever being precisely the same again. Sometimes things that are said leave marks which no apology can remove completely. Friendship is fraught with the danger of being at cross purposes. On the other hand, the need for both restraint and candor is also an opportunity for people to develop and grow as they anticipate each other's needs in various situations. When a friend tells us that we are at fault in some matter, we may be able to hear and accept a painful truth precisely because we are confident of their good will.

This concern for the welfare of a friend can sometimes cause us to tell the truth even at the risk of losing the friend. This may occur in situations in which what he or she is doing or plans to do we consider a serious mistake. For example, let us say that a person who is passed up for a promotion decides to resign his or her job. If resigning the job would hurt our friend badly, we may have to say that the person who was promoted instead really did have the edge, even at the risk of destroying a friendship. To risk the termination of a friendship in such circumstances is actually an act of friendship; it involves concern for another's welfare, and requires us to have enough detachment from our own desire for the friendship—and all that it means—to risk even its termination on occasions.

This brings us to another dilemma in friendship, the relation between freedom and dependence. The recognition of "otherness," as we saw in the first chapter, supplies a necessary element for both friendship and marriage to develop and prosper. It curtails our tendency to be possessive. Perfect love not only recognizes the independence of what is not oneself, but is also aware of how limited and insufficient every creature is. Both sides of perfect love, independence and dependence, are present in friendship, but in a distinctive combination. Friendship is voluntary, unlike kinship; it retains its voluntary character, unlike marriage. In a friendship, both people are free to lead their lives, pursue their goals, follow their interests apart from each other. But because friends are concerned with each other's welfare, friendship also implies mutual help. To some degree this limits the freedom of each to live their lives, pursue goals, and to follow interests. Friends then do not have complete liberty, not only because a certain amount of time must be devoted to each other—and usually gladly, because friends enjoy each other's company—but also because all of us need help from time to time. Friends are often glad to help each other. But there are limits to how much assistance can be given or expected without infringing on the freedom each person has to live his or her own life. Since some people are very reticent about asking for help under any circumstances, we cannot make it a rule always to wait for a friend to ask us for help *explicitly*. On the other hand, to offer help without being asked explicitly may be an intrusion and conflict with the right of friends to lead their own lives and pursue their own goals. We sometimes have to endure the pain of watching a friend getting into difficulties: "The hardest thing to do for someone that you love is to let them alone so they can hurt themselves, if it is necessary, or do what they want to do."[12] How friends balance the two requirements of respecting each other's liberty and of helping each other greatly affects the capacity of a friendship to grow and develop.

Another complication is that assistance must be a two-way street. If one person supplies all or most of the assistance, then the friendship usually deteriorates, and this one-sidedness is certainly a violation of friendship. But even mutual help has its pitfalls, since helping in every case of need can so limit people's freedom that friendship comes to resemble the obligations that go with close kinship or marriage. Not all people will balance the competing tendencies of non-interference and assistance the same way, but every friendship must come to terms with them. Unless the contrary pulls of freedom and dependence are properly balanced, a friendship can become distorted or even fail.

We have now identified some of the elements involved in friendship. Each is composed of competing tendencies which must be balanced in order for a friendship to develop and prosper. This requires the development of discernment and skill. First, some degree of equality must be present and maintained so that mutual interest will not die out. Second, each person's tastes, outlook, and convictions must be balanced with a tolerance for the other's tastes, outlook, and convictions. Third, a balance between openness and concealment, and between candor and sensitivity, must be found. Fourth, there must be a willingness to risk the friendship itself because of a genuine concern for each other's good. Fifth, a balance between freedom and assistance must be worked out. In every friendship, there must be some recognition of "otherness."

Although they share the dynamics we have just described, friendships between men and friendships between women are different. C.S. Lewis's account of friendship in *The Four Loves* assumes that they are; he discusses male friendship only, and remarks in passing that he has no idea what female friendship is like.[13] Aristotle's classic account of friendship also has only male friendship in mind.[14] Yet more modern empirical studies suggest some marked differences in friendships between men and friendships between women.[15] According to these, men tend to be sociable in the context of work, especially in working together on teams. They have numerous superficial friendships, a hail-fellow-well-met attitude, but show little trust and usually do not confide in their friends. Many men who have friends report that they do not and never have had a *close* friend. Much of this reflects the competitiveness among men in our society and the aversion to admitting and exposing weaknesses. Thus there is little personal sharing and emotional investment in their friendships, although men quite naturally stress shared activity. By contrast, women place a higher value on personal sharing and supportiveness, and so individual personality is more important. Shared activities are a vital part of female friendship too, but in contrast to men, they share in more spontaneous activity. As has been implied, women are more intimate in sharing themselves, and make friends less quickly and less extensively, but their friendships are deeper and more satisfying.

The role of women in our society is changing rapidly, however, and it will be interesting to see whether an increase in women's participation in vital parts of our political and economic system will affect the character of friendship among women. Their changing role has already had one visible effect: it has produced friendships between women and men. Although such friendships are still considered to be very unusual, nonetheless they do exist despite the many cultural expectations that interfere with such friendships. The most significant barrier is the dominance of the idea of romantic love. It is usually assumed that an interest in a person of the other sex is most properly a romantic interest. Should a case of a male-female friendship be encountered, it is assumed that something "higher" had been sought but not achieved. Male and female friends, because they spend time together, are frequently asked, "Why don't you get married?" or "When are you going to get married?"

It is also assumed that for either partner of a marriage to have a friend of the opposite sex is incompatible with the idea of marriage. In fact, friendships with a member of the *same* sex can even come to grief because of the hostility of a spouse, but it is almost impossible for a friendship with a member of the opposite sex to be sustained after one or the other friend gets married. It is much easier for people in a well-established marriage to make friends with a member of the opposite sex, especially if there is a significant age difference between the friends. But even here our cultural attitudes are heavily weighted against it. In our society it is assumed that a married couple ought to be "best friends," and that a spouse is able to meet all of their partner's emotional needs. This puts an enormous burden on marriage and is one of the reasons for so much unhappiness in marriage, as we shall see. But the existence of some male-female friendships, and the potential increase of such friendships because of the changing role of women in our society, suggests that we need to distinguish more than we have done so far between romantic love and friendship.

I have already mentioned that romantic love has a sexual element as an essential ingredient, while friendship does not. Romantic love also has an element of "brinkmanship," whereby people "play hard to get," an element which is out of place in friendship. Friendship is also generally far more serene and less turbulent than romantic love. People report that they find far more understanding from a friend than they do from a lover. Sexuality is of course part of a person and does affect a relationship, but in true friendship there is no overt sexual activity. This is evident in the rise of anxiety in those cases in which there is a transition from friends to "friend-lovers" because the stakes have changed, as I mentioned earlier.

The nature of male-female friendship is viewed quite differently by men and women. Men make a sharp distinction between their friendships with men and their friendships with women. Women do not. Men tend to regard their relations to women very uniformly; women are much more discriminating and generally evaluate each of their relationships individually. Men feel a responsibility to take the initiative and to assert their masculinity. They tend to seek in their friendship with women a refuge from the competitive pressures of male interaction, and as a result they have a tendency to use friendship with a woman as a *means* for finding the closeness they are afraid to seek with men; they may even seek to be "mothered." Men also may use friendship as a subtle springboard into sexual intimacy, since their view of women is dominated to a greater degree by the *theory* of romantic love, where women are viewed primarily as objects of erotic pleasure and havens of bliss. Women seem to have a superior capacity to manage their feelings and to distance themselves in their relations with men. So not only does male competitiveness restrict men's possibilities for close relations with men, but stereotyped notions of romantic love encourage a narrow view of women.[16]

Denis de Rougemont, whose work on romantic love has already been mentioned, considers that the *theory* of romantic love not only has placed an intolerable burden on marriage, but that by giving us a stereotyped view of the relation of men and women has prevented men from becoming mature enough to recognize women as individuals.[17] According to such a theory, women exist only to be passionately loved. Such love is supposed to be the most significant event in life, having a transcendent quality that raises one out of the mundane world and detaches the essence of one's self from all human affairs. This is symbolized in romantic stories with the ending, "And they lived happily ever after." With a romantic ideology, women are not considered as individuals, but are lumped together as beings possessed with the magical power to transport men out of their flat, dull world into a world of passionate delight. Men even consciously strive in our society to see a woman as merely an attractive or desirable body, and not as an independently existing person. Their reverie prevents them from taking in more than one aspect of a complete person. Erotic urges are turned into an obsession, whose supposed irresistibility excuses their attitudes and actions toward women.

What men assume to be dictated by their physical nature is actually something that has been largely learned. De Rougement believes that greater awareness on our part of the ideology of romantic love can bring great benefits not only to friendship and marriage, but to all male-female relations. An increased awareness can enable us to learn to meet and respond to people more as individuals, valuing them for their distinctive traits instead of assessing them for their potential for sexual activity. We shall examine this ideology more fully in the next chapter, and here I will only mention that it apparently affects men more than women. So for a friendship between a man and a woman to develop and prosper, an awareness not only of the dynamics present in all friendship is needed, but also of the effects of this particular ideology.[18] One of the potential values of friendship between the sexes is that it provides an opportunity for breaking an ideological hold, thus allowing us to act with more maturity in all female and male relations. But as long as stereotyped sexual attitudes remain *tacit*, friendships between men and women are especially vulnerable. In any friendship, but especially in those between the sexes, a shared view of what the relation means—its morality—is necessary. There are so few generally accepted guidelines in our society for friendship.

Consider, for example, an incident reported by Bertrand Russell in his autobiography.[19] Russell, in the course of describing his friendship with Alfred North Whitehead, mentions that Whitehead frequently neglected to give his wife enough money to run their household. Bill-collectors would hound his wife for payment, and occasionally Russell would give her some money to ease the situation. Whitehead, he says, never knew about it.

Whether this is or is not proper behavior for a friend is an interesting issue, but I am concerned here with the fact that Russell told the world about it. Was this a breach of the confidentiality to be expected in friendship? Whitehead was dead when Russell's autobiography appeared, but it seems to me that even this does not sanction the revelation. In friendship anything that could, if made public, be injurious to our friend's reputation ought to remain a private matter *forever*. Friendship inevitably involves an exposure of a great deal of our privacy to one who is trusted to maintain that privacy. A friend may share with others only what his or her friend would sanction, either implicitly or explicitly.

This is, however, *my* view of the nature of friendship. Should I learn that a friend of mine does not agree with me on this matter, it would affect what I chose to share from then on. It would lead me to be more guarded and so adversely affect the friendship. I find, however, that about half the people to whom I mention what Russell did do not agree with me. They believe that the public has the right to know everything about a person who is a public figure, as Whitehead was, and certainly after the person is dead.

We do not need to try to adjudicate this matter. The point is that people differ in their opinion, and that with each specific friendship the nature of confidentiality must be worked out. Otherwise a friendship can be injured, or even come to an end, on account of a difference of norms and the failure to make appropriate adjustments because of this difference.

Such differences arise in the case of every one of the elements of friendship we have discussed. People not only have different views about the relation of openness and confidentiality, but also over the place of candor in friendship, over how much assistance is appropriate or how much freedom or independence is to be exercised. All of these differences must be taken into account for a friendship to develop and prosper. The balance between each pair of tendencies in friendship—between independence and dependence, openness and concealment, candor and restraint—vary greatly in each specific friendship. One person may want to spend more time together than the other; one may be too dependent, and so hinder the other's freedom; one may feel prohibited from acting without consulting the other; one may feel obliged to act without consulting the other; one may have a need to provide assistance, but the other may feel that assistance should be given only when explicitly asked for; one may have the need to confide everything, the other may be more reluctant. These matters must be worked out between friends of either sex, but in friendships between men and women sexual stirrings and proper expressions of affection must also be dealt with. Some sexual interest is a factor that is quite likely to be present at least to some degree, even if only covertly.

It should now be obvious that friendship requires the development of considerable maturity. The number of opposing tendencies that must be balanced, and the voluntary nature of the relation itself, have always made it a difficult one to sustain. With our mobility today, friendship is even more difficult to maintain and develop. That is why it is vital for us to be more aware of what is requisite for our friendships to prosper, as well as to help prevent needless misunderstandings. Such examination also reveals the importance of the Christian virtue of forgiveness. Because there are so many pitfalls in friendship, forgiveness is necessary for them to be sustained. However well informed we may be about the dynamics of friendship, we are not fully in control of our needs and desires, even if we are very mature. We will injure each other. To be injured causes us to feel resentment and to desire revenge. We wish to exact from another person a recognition of our injury. Inflicting pain is one way to make another person take notice.

To feel resentment and to desire revenge is a perfectly natural reaction; we have been violated. But this reaction must be mitigated by a frank recognition that all of us violate other people. We must not only attend to the injury done to us, but also call to mind the fact that we too injure others. This recollection may help us to forgive. If we are in touch with divine love, we may find it even easier to forgive; we may also find ourselves less apt to feel resentment toward a friend who fails. The fact that we have been forgiven by God for our failures gives an incentive to forgive others. Divine love at work in us enables us to become more and more able to forgive. We can find ourselves without even a sense of resentment. We have a clear-eyed view of the harm done to us, and we can call a person's attention to the wrong they have done without rancor.

It is important to keep a proper balance between "nature and grace," that is, between human capacities and the addition made to these capacities by the influence of divine love. Grace helps us to forgive, but God's grace is not a substitute for developing the skills necessary for friendship to prosper. A Christian is not relieved of the necessity to show discretion with the self-revelations of a friend, for example. A Christian must learn how to balance candor and tenderness. A Christian must learn when and how to be honest, and not avoid the discipline of discernment by always going to the extreme of accepting in a permissive way all of a friend's attitudes and behavior. In short, a Christian must develop into a mature human being, and learn to exercise all the skills that every human being must exercise for friendships to develop and prosper. The assistance of divine grace cannot be made a substitute for our human responsibilities. On the other hand, because friendship requires a recognition of "otherness," whatever progress is made toward that religious goal contributes to the quality of friendship. A developing friendship may in turn increase our capacity to love our neighbor. In fact, we can love a neighbor in the person of a friend.

With these remarks about the interactions of "grace and nature," I have completed my remarks on the nature of friendship. So far I have not touched on the nature of homosexual friendship, but as an issue it is so important that I will try to say something about it here. The issue is complex because it involves biblical teachings, different ethical perspectives, and also the human sciences. To use these sources involves problems of biblical interpretation, some knowledge of different theories of ethics, and a sensitivity to the fact that the human sciences are not exact sciences like physics and chemistry. In addition there are issues of discrimination and civil rights. But I can say enough about homosexuality here to indicate why I treat the norm of sexual love as heterosexual. It will not settle, much less treat, all the issues, but it will explain why I discuss friendship as a non-sexual relation and treat romantic love and marriage in heterosexual terms only.

It is commonly claimed today that our bias toward heterosexual love is a matter only of social norms. I have often heard it said that homosexuality was socially acceptable among the ancient Greeks, for example, although as matter of fact it was accepted only in special circumstances. In his authoritative work on education, Henri Marrou claims that the Greeks had a distinctive educational institution whereby an older man took responsibility for the moral and social education of an adolescent. The insitution was initially developed in an earlier warrior culture, and by the time of Socrates and Plato it was gradually being replaced by a more formal education which no longer concerned itself with the transmission of martial virtues. But all later educational systems retained some elements of the powerful attachment between warrior and apprentice. That attachment was a profound and deep love which, in some cases at least, included homosexual acts. But homosexuality was not encouraged or even generally approved of outside this educational institution.[20] Homosexual acts certainly occurred, but one of Plato's characters in the *Symposium* claims that it is such improper practices which have given the homosexual love between boy and man a bad name.[21] Plato himself (and Aristotle as well) did not approve of such sexual acts, even in the institutionalized form. Thus, although homosexuality was practiced in ancient Greece, it was accepted in one institutional context only; even there, it was not accepted by major representatives of the society.

Nor can the attitudes of Roman society in the apostle Paul's time be used to support homosexuality. There was promiscuous self-indulgence by people in nearly every aspect of life, including heterosexual and homosexual activity. Acceptance of homosexuality by many Romans took place in a context where there were few ethical standards at all.

Martin Opler, a professor of social psychiatry and anthropologist who has worked among the Ute Indians, concludes after reviewing many major studies of various societies that "no society, save perhaps ancient Greece, pre-Meiji Japan, certain top echelons in Nazi Germany, and the scattered examples of such special status groups as the berdaches, Nata slaves, and one category of Churkchee shamans, has lent sanction in any real sense to homosexuality."[22] Yet at the same time we find in an authoritative denominational study the statement, "The majority of societies that have been studied have condoned homosexual behavior."[23]

A claim for homosexuality which should be taken more seriously than these is based on a theory of human development. According to classic psychoanalytic theory, human beings' sexual interest is highly plastic and non-specific in infancy. It is not innately patterned toward either male or female objects, but only gradually through socialization becomes oriented one way or the other. This theory, and those studies which support it, are sometimes used to claim that homosexuality is an equal pattern of sexual practice and on a par with heterosexual marriage. Don Browning, a professor of pastoral theology and counseling, however, points out some of the limitations of this argument. It assumes that because there is no innate pattern of sexual preference, all parental and social values and needs with respect to preference are to be dropped; human beings are to be allowed to find their own way, uninstructed.[24] Yet Browning thinks that this same data can be used to make quite a different point:

> Because of our sexual malleability, the direction cultures give to our sexuality is determined by the need to balance our sexual tendencies with the whole range of other vital human tendencies and needs. Indeed, it is precisely because our sexual nature can go easily in a variety of directions for expression—toward homosexuality, bisexuality, or heterosexuality—that culture helps to shape it for us in certain ways. Historically, the ways in which culture has shaped sexuality have been designed to adjust our sexual tendencies and needs harmoniously with other vital—and sometimes even conflicting—tendencies and needs. . . . Diffuse homosexual and bisexual activity may increasingly have been experienced as a threat to the stability of other vital values. Heterosexual and covenanted marriage may have emerged as the preferred method for patterning sexuality precisely because it managed to organize and actualize justly a wider range of potentially conflicting tendencies and needs.[25]

Browning goes on to argue that homosexuality can serve several human needs and values. Casual homosexual relations convey only pleasure. Stable long-term ones not only give sexual pleasure, but provide security, a measure of consistent identity, and help bind a couple into a cooperative unit that helps with the practical tasks of life. But covenanted heterosexual organization of sexuality provides these things and *more*, including the values to be found in having children, and sharing intergenerational values throughout life. In addition, Browning uses these social facts to argue that heterosexual marriage is *morally* superior. On this basis he concludes that other forms of organizing sexuality are to be tolerated—homosexuals are to have full civil rights—but they are not to be *advocated*. Homosexuality should not be given equal status with covenanted heterosexuality. "The basic symbols, rituals, energies, and practical rules of the church should, as in the past, be put to the service of covenanted heterosexuality."[26]

If this approach continues to be accepted, then it means that those people who are homosexuals or who have homosexual tendencies are going to find themselves, as they are now, bucking social and moral norms. Quite naturally this will create serious problems for many of them. Therefore we must be ready to show them the same sort of consideration we show to all people who by reason of predisposition, temperament, upbringing, or choice go against prevailing social or moral norms. They are all too easily victimized, misrepresented, and treated unfairly. In particular we must remember that individuals of any group that is socially unacceptable tend to internalize the social rejection by developing self-hatred and self-loathing. The resulting suffering can be immense.

This discussion of homosexuality is really an excursion from our main topic, and it does not pretend to be a complete account of the issue. But given our widespread consciousness of it today, some discussion of it could not be avoided in an examination of friendship.

Finally, we need to look at the particular bond between Christians which is neither friendship nor love of neighbor. It is sometimes referred to as *koinonia*, or fellowship, in the New Testament. *Koinonia* is distinct from love of neighbor because it is a mutual or a two-sided relation; love of neighbor may be one-directional and not reciprocated.[27] We are to love our neighbor because of our common creaturehood and the image of God, which we all share. *Koinonia* includes these, but it also has other ingredients, as we shall see.

Koinonia is distinct from friendship. We should not be misled by John 15:14, where Jesus calls the disciples "friends." It is clear in this passage that he does not mean friendship as we have considered it, because Jesus gives as a condition, "If you do what I command you." In the context in which Jesus is speaking of his disciples as his friends, he is contrasting the status slaves occupy to the status of his disciples. They are to be obedient, but not blindly obedient. He has disclosed to them all that he has heard from his Father. In addition, the commandment the disciples are to obey is "to love one another." They are Jesus' "friends," associated with him and each other because he himself obeys the commandment, and indeed obeys it perfectly, because he will lay down his life for them.

The bond in friendship initially lies usually in common pursuits, and it grows into the mutual love of two people. Friendship is primarily based on "nature," that is, on our natural human endowments, in contrast to the specific divine grace or love which comes (whether recognized or not) from God, and works in our lives to overcome our egocentrism. *Koinonia*, on the other hand, includes all Christians. The bond is not natural attraction, one to another, but the grace of God that issues in faith in Jesus Christ and love for God. For *koinonia* to develop and prosper, not only must divine grace be operative in us, but we must also exercise our natural powers to learn some of the same skills that are necessary for friendship, such as discretion. In fact, one of the problems with Christian fellowship is that people may rely solely on the bond of divine grace and so neglect the need to develop ordinary good manners, as well as a good character.

There is also a strong tendency among Christians towards utopianism, because they are aware of the power of divine love to improve us. But it is a mistake to ignore the power and strength of our distorted and fallen human nature. We must learn what Reinhold Niebuhr called "Christian realism." On the one hand we must avoid the pitfalls of utopianism, which seems to be present in so much of present-day social action, and on the other hand we must not become cynical when we find that, all too often, church life is hardly distinct from that of a social club.

It is important to distinguish friendship from Christian fellowship or *koinonia* because friendship is often held up as the standard for the way church members ought to be related to each other, especially in American parish life. Yet it is false and unrealistic to expect large numbers of people to be friends. Such a standard can make people feel guilty for their imagined shortcomings, or lead to false friendliness among church people. It can also lead us to overlook the distinctive nature of Christian fellowship. *Koinonia* is itself an important and vital bond, and to be cultivated properly it needs to be distinguished from friendship. Let us look briefly at its nature.

The church is the context for Christian fellowship. The word "church" in the New Testament is *ekklesia*, which in Greek simply means "assembly." When used in the New Testament, however, it has several specific meanings. In the first place, the assembly is the "people of God." The earliest Christians were conscious of the fact that they were a new Israel. They had ties to the covenant God made with Abraham, but in Christ a new covenant had been formed. The people of God were no longer to be thought of as a nation, or as having an ethnic identity; there was no earthly distinction which excluded anyone from Christian fellowship. The common bond is an attachment to the crucified and risen Lord. *Koinonia* is an expression of the common life Christians share. "What we have seen and heard we declare to you, so that you and we together may share in a common life, that life which we share with the Father and his Son Jesus Christ" (I John 1:3-4).[28]

Christian fellowship is a distinctive love, then, because it reaches across all earthly barriers and distinctions. As Paul says, "There is neither Jew nor Greek, there is neither slave nor free, there is neither male nor female; for you are all one in Christ Jesus" (Gal. 3:28). Because of Christ, we are able to transcend these differences sufficiently to share in a fellowship with each other. There is a particular joy to be found in sharing with others in worship; it is elevating to speak and hear and direct our hearts and minds to what all of us love.

Koinonia includes suffering. Christ our Lord suffered for our redemption, and our participation in that suffering means that we care about the suffering of all people. One part of Christian fellowship or love is to take responsibility for people who suffer; another is to use our gifts and talents for the service to others. Hence in Protestantism there has been a stress on the vocation of all Christians to serve others in their work. Finally, Christian ministry is the acceptance of a responsibility to spread the life that is to be found in and through Christ to others. Christian fellowship has only been partially realized. This should not be too surprising. When we consider how difficult it is for friendship to be realized and sustained, a relationship that involves only two people, it is remarkable how much—rather than how little—Christian fellowship is practiced.

Christian fellowship, then, is a genuine bond, but it is not friendship. This is important to realize, because sometimes the shared life of the parish church can become oppressive. If we think that *koinonia* is the same as friendship, then we may press people to take part in the many activities of the church. But some people may not want to be involved in this way. In fact, some people are driven away from church attendance precisely because of the pressure to take part in many activities in which they are not interested and which are not specifically connected to the Christian life. They may, of course, also fail to accept their share of the responsibility for the common life of the church. But my intention here is not to define what are and what are not specifically Christian activities. It is instead to free us of a false standard of what Christian fellowship is. It is not friendship, and thus does not have the responsibilities of friendship. People can be perfectly good members of the church and part of its fellowship, and still not be friends.

Friendship is a specific kind of bond. It is neither *koinonia* nor love of neighbor. For it to grow and develop, many skills and personal qualities such as tolerance and candor must be cultivated, as we have already seen. Yet at bottom friendship, like every other relationship, requires us to become progressively more free of our confining and distorting egocentricity, so that we can recognize and love "otherness." Divine love, even when unacknowledged, quietly and secretly seeks to open us to a fuller life, one of whose greatest ornaments is friendship.

Love seeketh not itself to please,
Nor for itself hath any care,
But for another gives its ease,
And builds a heaven in hell's despair

Love seeketh only self to please,
To bind another to its delight,
Joys in another's loss of ease,
And builds a hell in heaven's despite.

William Blake, *Songs of Experience*

Romantic Love and Marriage

Education is supposed to prepare us for life, but it has not prepared us to deal with romantic love very well. So much of our life is affected by unrealistic and even contradictory ideas about love; to take a harder look at what we mean by romantic love is a matter of practical common sense. It is not easy to say what romantic love is, because our ideas have changed over a period of time, nor do we have any authoritative text to refer to, as we do when we seek to say what a Platonic or a Christian understanding of love is. In spite of these difficulties, however, we may specify at least what some of its main features are. Romantic love is love between a man and a woman, and such love is thought to be one, if not the, way to human fullfillment. Yet a major theme in literature is that romantic love is the cause of tragedy. In Virgil's *Aenead*, Dido falls hopelessly in love with Aeneas, who must leave her in order to lead the Trojans to Italy where they will found the city of Rome. In despair she kills herself. This connection between love and death is also found in Shakespeare's *Anthony and Cleopatra* and *Romeo and Juliet*.

To a considerable extent today romantic love, which for us is supposed to be the main reason for getting married, still carries an undertone of the incompatibility of romance and marriage, an idea that originated with the medieval troubadours. In Tolstoy's novel Anna Karenina, for example, true love springs up between a woman who is already married and another man. After a struggle, *Anna Karenina* chooses love over marriage and her child, but since her situation is impossible, she kills herself. Many twentieth-century novels share Tolstoy's theme, although the outcome may be less drastic. We will look into the supposed incompatibility of romantic love and marriage at length later on.

We also find romantic love portrayed in many love stories as a slave-like adoration of man and woman for each other. It is an all-consuming passion, with overtones of a sacred union of souls; for romantic love often stresses that love ennobles both lover and beloved and that their passion for one another, though sexual, transcends mere libidinal impulse.

With the rise of industrialization and the increase of commercial activity in the nineteenth century, many people came to feel that the romance of life had been lost. There developed a restless romantic searching for something that would restore high feelings and passion in a world that had become commonplace, petty, and meaningless. Not only did tragic love become a favorite theme in literature, music, and art, so also a falling in love with love itself increasingly became a preoccupation. There was an urgent longing for, and belief in, the powerful passion that would sweep people off their feet and restore vitality. The individual love object, male or female, hardly mattered.

Perhaps a series of catch-words collected by Thomas Gould, one of the best contemporary writers on Plato's view of love, gives the flavor of our view of romantic love today better than these references to literature.

> If two people love each other, nothing else matters. . . .
> Love prevents even adulterous sex from being really
> immoral. . . . A man who loses everything for a love,
> even an illicit love, is to be both pitied and envied . . .
> For a woman . . . it is immoral . . . not to do everything
> in her power to make men have erotic desires whenever
> they look at her, and if she does not have at least one

man at any given time who adores her, her life is pointless. . .[29]

But these ideas have not prevented people, at least until very
recently, from also holding to this romantic view at the same time:

> The natural expectation of every boy and girl is that
> each will fall in love, once, in the bloom of youth, sud-
> denly, intensely, and at first unhappily, desiring infinitely
> more than sexual fulfillment but desiring that as well;
> that each will fall in love with a person of the opposite
> sex, also young and beautiful, who is unattached and
> falls just as much in love in return; that they will marry
> and experience a bliss which cannot even be talked
> about.[30]

Nonetheless romantic love itself, in contrast to these ideas
about it, is not to be dismissed entirely. The problem is a lack of realism in our ideas concerning love between man and woman, a lack
of realism that can be destructive. For example, if we believe the
idea that love between men and women cannot last, so that a life-
long commitment such as marriage calls for is to be avoided, we
create enormous problems for children, who need security and a
great deal of care if they are to become healthy and responsible
adults. This idea tends to undermine the stability of society, which
must often assume responsibility for the emotionally disturbed
children of broken marriages. If too many marriages fail, a society
may be hard-pressed to maintain itself.

Apart from these considerations, the idea that love cannot
endure, or is unlikely to, causes a great deal of anxiety for the partners of a marriage. This anxiety is compounded by the idea that,
should a married person either fall out of love or fall in love with

someone else, it would be wrong for him or her to continue the marriage. This is a compelling idea not only because life is assumed to be pointless without romantic love, it is considered virtually a sacred duty to leave a spouse in the name of "love." Such an attitude has been reinforced by popular distortions of Freud, the notion that I must be good to myself because the suppression of my needs will do me great mental harm and that the fear of pursuing personal pleasure is the result of merely a rigid conscience.

This belief that there is an emotion which is to be desired above all else, and for which all else is to be sacrificed because without it one has not lived, can lead to a fruitless "Don Quixote" quest—a search for what does not exist—and so distort one's relations to all members of the opposite sex. Many married people, if asked whether they love their spouse, are likely to feel guilty. This is not because they do not love their spouses, but because they lack the sentiment they think they are supposed to have, largely thanks to the way love is portrayed in films, magazines, books, and popular talk. Lovers are all extraordinary people. The woman has beauty, charm, and allure. The man is handsome, virile, and masterful. When such extraordinary people come within range of each other, they are supposed to be possessed by a flame and swept by an uncontrollable ardour. Now if a man's wife is not even pretty, much less dazzling, how is he to be in love that way? Nor are most husbands handsome, virile-looking, and masterful. How then is a flame to be ignited in a woman's soul? Love may be blind, but how blind can it be when the wife is fifty-two years old, with dyed hair and a body that sags in all the wrong places, and when the husband is fifty-five years old, bald, and with breath that always smells of garlic?

It is no accident that romantic love stories are portrayed by Hollywood faces and figures. Yet most people who marry are ordinary people. If many of them do love each other, it is not in the admired and supposedly archetypical way. According to this understanding of love, most of us are doomed never to have lived all. Furthermore, it is implied that should we have the requisite physical equipment, but nonetheless not have been seared by the flame of love or torn apart by a frenzy, then something must be wrong with us. Perhaps in that case we need to read D.H. Lawrence in order to learn how civilization has destroyed our vital energies and how we need to be liberated from the deadening effects of reason. But perhaps the truth lies more nearly with Virginia Woolf's comment, "He was not 'in love,' of course; it was one of those unclassified affections of which there are so many."[31] Many ordinary people do love each other, but genuine love between men and women is too specific to each individual case, as we shall see, to be adequately captured by the feelings Hollywood faces and figures evoke.

It is also highly unrealistic and dangerous to rely on any single emotion to give happiness or to be the only road to salvation. Too many people who indeed approximate the model of romantic love, and who are powerfully moved by another person, learn that such an emotion is not enough to carry them through all the challenges of life. It is not even enough to meet all the challenges of dealing fruitfully with the beloved. As the quotation from Blake's poem cited at the beginning of this chapter suggests, love can lead to a heavenly or hellish situation. But we should not isolate the way we feel from the rest of ourselves. A person has purposes or goals, an outlook on life, and a formed or unformed character. The way a person feels and treats another person is affected deeply for good or ill by these factors. They determine whether a person's love for another person is elevating and edifying, or degrading and destructive. They affect the quality and nature of love, as we shall see.

What is needed today is a more realistic view of romantic love; that is, the love between men and women needs to be liberated from many destructive ideas. We need to see what love can actually achieve. I myself am not ready to dismiss romantic love completely, as are people who have become cynical because so many of our ideas about it are unrealistic. Romantic love can be stripped of its extravagances, seen more clearly for what it can and cannot do, by being looked at in the context of marriage. For the institution of marriage enables the love a man and a woman feel for each other to achieve its *own* ends: to love well, always, and faithfully. The emotion itself cannot achieve its own ends. The emotion leads to weal or woe because of the kinds of people we are. Nor can the emotion of love itself guarantee that we shall love another always; we are all only too familiar with the way people fall into and out of love. Nor does being in love of itself keep our eyes and desires from wandering to another person. Marriage as an institution can greatly help to form our character so that we can love well, always, and faithfully. Marriage is not anti-thetical to love, as some views of romantic love claim, but an institution which can enable the love two people have for each other to achieve what love seeks.

Most of the factors that help friendship to grow and prosper—tolerance, and a balance between openness and respecting privacy, candor and sensitivity, freedom and assistance—also help romantic love to become more realistic and so achieve its ends. Since we have discussed them already, we shall here treat only those additional factors needed for the development of a realistic romantic love between men and women.

Irving Singer, the philosopher mentioned earlier, promises to give us a realistic view of romantic love in the next volume of his trilogy, *The Nature of Love*. In the two previously published volumes he claims that Christian love ("agape") does not include love between persons because it teaches us that God is the ultimate source of love; human beings are neither the source of love nor worthy objects of love. However far-fetched this seems at first sight, Singer has simply followed Anders Nygren's influential account of Christian love in *Agape and Eros* to its logical conclusion. The issues are numerous and complex, but we can say that both writers have limited Christian love to giving, with the result that to seek to *receive* under any circumstance is regarded as selfish. Since in human love we frequently desire to receive, Nygren dismisses all human loves as un-Christian. He even claims that to combine Christian love with human love in any way is an unmitigated corruption of Christian love. But Singer, on the same basis, dismisses Christianity altogether for its inability to find a place for love between persons.[32]

In his survey of Christian writers on romantic love, however, Singer fails to mention that Soren Kierkegaard, a major nineteenth-century writer, has already given an account of love between man and woman. By so doing, Kierkegaard has modified the notion of romantic love in such a way as to make it more realistic. In addition, Kierkegaard has related love between man and woman to Christian love in a very positive way. Since Kierkegaard has given a realistic view of romantic love by connecting romantic love to the institution of marriage, we shall draw upon his account, especially his essay "The Aesthetic Validity of Marriage," found in the second volume of *Either/Or*.[33]

The word "aesthetic" in the title of his essay is used by Kierkegaard in a special sense. It refers to a particular kind of outlook on life. An aesthete is neither ethical nor religious. According to Kierkegaard, all of us are born aesthetes, and only become ethical or religious people by *choosing* to do so. Much of Kierkegaard's writings are an account of how this transition may take place. To become an ethical person is not so much a choice in the first instance between good *or* evil, but rather the choice between taking into consideration good and evil on the one hand, and the exclusion of *both* of them from consideration on the other. An aesthete has either avoided making that choice, or explicitly chosen not to recognize the priority of obligation over one's own wishes, desires, and inclinations. An aesthete judges all things on the basis of their being *interesting*. The stance and attitude toward all objects, events, and people is that they either provide interest or they don't. The world is divided into these two categories, and they are all that matters. It is only a question of, "Is it interesting to me?" The aesthete wants to be fascinated, thrilled, excited, entertained to such an extent that this need dominates a whole life.

The aesthete's personality has other characteristics, too, and for our purposes the best way to bring them out is to see the example of an aesthete in action. This example is taken from the novel, *An Unofficial Rose*, by Iris Murdoch.[34] It presents the story of an aesthete who is already married, and shows how he views self-fullfillment, or happiness.

The main plot concerns this man, named Randall, who together with his wife runs a rose nursery garden. It is a modestly successful business. But as the novel opens, the wife is doing all the work. She prepares the catalogue for the printer, sees to the mailing, manages the working of the garden, looks after the children, and the like. Randall has become immobile; he is no longer interested in roses, in breeding new types, in the challenge of founding a business. His wife Ann bores him beyond description. He just sits in his office all day thinking of how he can escape from this drab, confining, monotonous, pointless life. He feels trapped and bound by the nursery garden and by a wife who is simply ordinary—indistinguishable from any other woman.

But there is still a spark of fire in Randall. There is a luscious beauty in his life who makes everything worthwhile. The world becomes "interesting" when she is in the picture. But she is accessible only under certain conditions. The woman is willing to go off with Randall, in fact she is quite keen on the idea, but only if and when he gets some money, and a lot of money at that. She wants money to live in style, money to travel, money in order to be somebody.

There are other ramifications to the story, but finally Randall gets some money by badgering his aging father to sell a valuable painting. Like the Prodigal Son, he demands his inheritance. Off he goes with his mistress to Rome—to a marvelous, glamorous life. He and his mistress are free of all daily routines and obligations, free to indulge their sensuous desires, and free at last to be themselves.

This tale is as ordinary as a soap-opera, indeed as ordinary as life itself. It is about the ordinary desire to live extraordinarily, the desire of the aesthete to escape from what is common and normal. Here it takes the form of a person who wants to be free of the everyday, free to be himself—which in this case means to be free to follow his own interests, moods and desires. Randall was once interested in Ann, his wife. At one time their love of roses and the challenge of founding a business together was a thrilling goal, an adventure. But then he changed. Why should he be bound to a dead past? Why should he deny all that was vital and alive in himself? Why should he remain in bondage? His marriage did not hold out any hope of a future for him or for Ann. Why remain bound and suppress his own person, his own potential for happiness, his own individuality? Life should be exciting, full of beauty and sparkle. And he knew where that could be found. All that stood in his way was Ann—good, old, dull, faithful Ann—more predictable, he thought, than a loyal dog. Only Ann and a lack of money blocked him from freedom and happiness.

Randall represents a common idea of self-fullfillment, of freedom, and of the true expression of oneself. To be an individual means to be able to express one's in-built wishes and desires, which for most of us include sexual and sensuous desires. This idea assumes that it is our wishes and desires that make us *individuals*. So we believe that it is only a lack of money, or only our obligations to others, that keep us from realizing our own individuality.

For Kierkegaard, however, this is a mistaken idea of what it is to be an individual. Randall is not a master of himself at all. Such a person lives an *accidental* life, that is, a life based on the accidents of temperament and the desires which drive him. His endowment determines his life. He has to alter the course of his life whenever those desires change. Randall once loved roses; he no longer loves roses. He once loved Ann; Ann is no longer exciting to him—though as a matter of fact, she is desired by two other people. One of them is a professional soldier, dashing and rich to boot, who adores Ann precisely for the very qualities that bore Randall. For the problem is not Ann; it is the fact that Randall has changed. His immediate sensuous desires, as well as his ideas about glamorous romance, direct and control him. This is evident both from Randall's cheap promiscuity (for he is easily prey to casual sex) and from his attitude toward his mistress after they get to Rome. Just when they are at last free to run away, finally able to realize their ideal of a glamorous, extravagant life together, we find Randall at the summit of his achievement musing over the beauty of his sleeping mistress: "I'll get tired of her one day, but it does not matter. There are lots of other beautiful women."

He will become bored with her, too, because he has no power or mastery over his own interests or infatuations. But it is all right, he thinks, the external world will always provide him with variety that will keep life interesting and boredom at bay. Someone like

71

Randall depends on what is *external* in order to live, rather than having the internal power to direct his life in a satisfactory way with a significant degree of independence from external circumstances. He will find it harder and harder to build the dream of idyllic, thrilling love and a glamorous life with each succeeding person, even should he manage to continue to have the money to afford high living. Boredom is already surfacing within a few weeks of this adventure.

Randall is not, then, an individual; he has no significant control over his own life. Individuality, or genuine character, cannot be built on the basis of the given endowment of our sensuous nature, temperament, or accidental interests. Unless we achieve self-direction, we are fated to be driven by these other and more destructive forces. We are forced to arrange external circumstances in order to gratify them. We are following Hume's famous formula, "Reason is and ought to be a slave of the passions," and by passions he does not mean merely sexual desires, but all that pushes, drives, and moves us. This is to live with the Freudian conception of an ego (our rational, conscious self) that serves to secure the drives of the id (our innate unconscious desires) in order to maximimize gratification. But the id decides and determines what we are to seek; we have no control over it. For Kierkegaard, to be an individual means to take responsibility for oneself, to become accountable for one's life.

To become an individual, one must choose to become a responsible person. This is done by deciding to recognize the validity of the category of obligation, and its priority over all else. Consequently we can direct our lives by an allegiance to what is permanent, rather than having to put our trust in what fluctuates uncontrollably. Obligations give shape and direction to the use of our endowment, and control over our desires. We cease to be aesthetes by making ourselves accountable for what we are, rather than remaining at the mercy of endowment, desires, whims, moods, external events. They lead to boredom, a boredom which requires constant change and variety in order to be held at bay. Randall's life has at its bottom the principle, "Vanity of vanities ... all is vanity." This woman or the next—it really does not matter. Although it does not matter, Randall cannot stop. Although his way does not make sense of life, it is the only way he can live now. Rather than finding love, finding himself, he has become a person who is increasingly incapable of love.

But there is a way of life and an outlook on life which does make sense, so that all is not in vain. This way is to live in the domain of the ethical. The ethical brings order and stability, direction and value to daily, ordinary life. It gives us goals which cause life to increase in richness, as we wrestle with the ups and downs of achieving them. The sensuous and the exciting find their place within a life that has validity, rather than becoming so important that we have no way to deal with daily life. Rather than always being under the need to escape from daily life, and the ever-recurring boredom which haunts those who have not come to terms with it, we can gain mastery over ourselves. The key is the recognition and acceptance of the reality of the domain of obligation as such.

The very word "obligation" sounds terrible in the ears of a person like Randall. It sounds like the announcement of death itself. What could be more terrible, more dull, more destructive of freedom and self-fullfillment than obligation? But Kierkegaard claims that it is only by entering the domain of the ethical that one can find mastery over the flux of desires, external events, the haunting spectre of boredom, and a life that lacks validity. One place where Kierkegaard seeks to show the soundness of his claims is in the obligations of marriage. Let us then examine Kierkegaard's essay, "The Aesthetic Validity of Marriage," and see how he makes good his claim.

This essay is supposedly written by the Judge, who represents the ethical outlook on life. The essay's title is ironic, for in it the aesthetic approach to life is repudiated. But the Judge seeks to show that romantic love, which the aesthete endorses, can achieve its ends not by the rejection of the validity of obligation, but precisely by its acceptance.

The essay takes the form of a letter that has supposedly been sent by the Judge to an aesthete, in which the Judge contrasts the aesthetic and ethical views of love and marriage. The aesthete enjoys falling in love, but he also knows that the thrill of love does not last. So far as he is concerned, falling in love is splendid, but married life, once the glow of love has faded, is bound to be boring, a trap to be avoided wherever possible. Love is spontaneous. It should be allowed expression with whomever one falls in love with, and not be confined, restricted, or suppressed by marriage.

The Judge maintains, however, that marriage is not inimical to the love between man and woman, but precisely what enables love to achieve what it seeks—but by itself it is incapable of attaining. The reason why marriage looks dull, and why the obligation it forms seems like a stranglehold, lies in the character of the aesthete, not in the institution of marriage. To a person who lives in the domain of the ethical, marriage is an adventure—rich, exciting, and fullfilling. Marriage can liberate a person from a life to which someone like Randall is condemned by his own weakness, and it can unite the spontaneity of love to the demands of duty. By this combination one is able in marriage to preserve and enhance love between a man and a woman. To make his case, the Judge contrasts an aesthetic view of love and marriage to an ethical view of each.

The points of contrast are many. But the underlying reason for the sharp differences between the two views is that the aesthete abhors commitment, while the ethical person endorses it. The aesthete is convinced that there are no joys which last. Sooner or later they pass, and so to commit oneself is to be doomed to a harvest of dullness. Consequently we are to avoid investing ourselves too fully in anyone; we are to keep our options open. If we do get married, we are to be ready to pull out when the marriage goes sour or when we find someone else who is more interesting.

The ethical outlook, on the other hand, *requires* commitment. One is to become bound. The ethical person can do this because he or she knows that there are some joys which do endure. There are some joys which are unknown to the aesthete precisely because the aesthete will not accept commitment, will not accept obligations. Rather than passing with time, there are some joys that actually increase. Instead of growing less, they become greater. But in order for us to find this out, we must undertake an obligation, in order for our joys to be realized.

The blindness of the aesthete is typified by romantic stories. In so-called "love stories" we have tales of a great adventure in which a lover fights his way through terrible odds and great danger to his beloved, and then the story ends with the phrase, "They lived happily ever after." However, Kierkegaard's Judge says that the story ends where it ought to *begin*, with their being together in happiness. Why is their happiness not portrayed in the story? Why is it we always get a description of the thrilling adventure of overcoming hazards, with the lovers finally sinking into one another's arms, and then the curtain falls, the book ends, and the viewer or reader is none the wiser about what happiness is. The excitement was in the striving, in the passionate desire to have the wish fulfilled. Now it is all over. There is nothing left to portray. If the wish is so wonderful as to be worth all the struggle, why is life with the beloved not described?

If one is to deal with the subject of love, one must not end with the glow and thrill of falling in love. There is more to experience. Marriage is the friend and developer of love. Here is an example that I recently came upon in my reading, which describes such a relationship:

> Every summer for as far back as I could remember, I had watched Robert and Mary Jones walking down the beach to the water for a swim. . . . A slightly comical couple because of their difference in size, they would walk at a leisurely pace, several feet apart, conversing. I never overheard much of what they said, but it was apparent that the conversation ranged from serious discussion to banter. Often it was punctuated with laughter. . . Their enjoyment of each other was arresting—sharp as pepper, golden. I have seen other happy old couples, but this picture of the Joneses, renewed many times, came to represent to me an essence of human exchange—sometimes indescribably moving and precious, which comes to fruition only toward the end of a lifelong marriage. Whatever that essence is, I find it dazzling. It has always struck me as one of the great possibilities life has to offer.[35]

The Judge in Kierkegaard's essay shows how one of life's great possibilities can be realized. He does not claim that every marriage is happy, but rather that the institution of marriage, which involves commitment, allows the realization of love between a man and a woman. He presents his case by contrasting an aesthetic view of love and marriage to an ethical view. Here are some of the points of contrast.

First, the aesthete considers the period of the couple's engagement to be better than the time of marriage. Falling in love, courtship, buying the ring, planning the wedding—that is the excitement. Then, afterwards, things become humdrum and routine.

The Judge, who represents the ethical outlook, considers marriage to be more beautiful than an engagement. Marriage means a commitment to a person who, as time goes on, will unfold more and more of him or herself, unfold the whole range of a human personality. You are to come to love *that* person, one who cannot be known in the brief period of an engagement. Compared to marriage, an engagement is but an anticipation of knowing and loving another.

Of this lifelong process of coming to understand both oneself and the other through the stability of marriage, a modern historian of ideas writes:

> It is no mean task to understand the deepest needs of one's self or of another. The most complete form of interpersonal love is found in marriage, for there the widest range of needs are involved, from the simple needs of food, clothing, and shelter, to the infinitely complex sexual, generative, emotional, and spiritual needs. The lifelong intimacy of marriage provides the best opportunity for probing interaction of deep interpersonal love; and its lifelong commitment is the most thorough expression of the benevolence of interpersonal love.[36]

But what if we find we do not like what is progressively revealed of another person? This brings us to the second point of contrast: two different understandings of the nature of love. The word "love" to the aesthete means a pleasant feeling. It takes no effort. Its hallmark is inconstancy. You fall into love and you fall out of it. You can love several people at once.

Yet Kierkegaard's Judge does not use the word that way, nor does he toss it around lightly. He uses it rarely, and with care and reverence. It is a feeling, but a feeling filled and anchored to an obligation. The obligation is not wholly external to the feeling. When genuine love begins, *if it is not merely sensual*, one recognizes in it an obligation *always* to love. Obligation is not tacked on to love, but rather is present in it from the start, unless it is a mere sensual glow or self-indulgence. Love itself includes a couple's resolve to meet the whole range of life together, even when there are days, months, and maybe years of pain, frustration, misunderstanding, and temptations.

According to the Anglican theologian and novelist Charles Williams, the experience of love is not a mere feeling, but has within it purpose or intention. The fulfillment of a purpose engages the mind and will. We can with our minds perceive those needs, tendencies, and desires which are destructive to our purpose to love another forever. We can by our will make the effort to detach ourselves progressively from whatever is a hindrance to our purpose to love another always. Because our love has an inherent intention, the mind and will can be used to understand both oneself and the beloved, and to seek to order emotions and other tendencies that enable this love to continue and to develop. We are not completely at the mercy of a love that comes and goes as it will, as is the case with the aesthete's kind of love.[37]

When the purpose to love always is inherent in love, and is accompanied by the resolve that goes with the commitment of marriage, we are sustained by the conviction that love can be preserved as more and more of each partner's character is unveiled. The very vocabulary that goes with married love indicates this: faithful, constant, humble, patient, long-suffering, indulgent, sincere, contented, vigilant, willing, joyful. All these words point to the *character* of a person. If we love this way, we do not fight dragons or villains, as in "love stories," but fight with ourselves, as more and more of ourself and our partner is revealed with time and through the ups and downs of life. We face an inward struggle with what we are. What is won is oneself and the other. Married people *become* people who love each other. They develop a shared life, a life that belongs to both. Such a becoming has a constancy and durability that cannot be reduced to a mere pleasant feeling that wells up one day and is no longer there the next.

If one should ask, "Why get married?" the aesthete would answer that it is not a good idea. It would be better always to be young, single, and dashing about. An ethical person cannot give a good reason for marriage, either. It is certainly not in order to have a home, nor to have children. How comic it would be to say to our beloved, "Let us get married because I want to have a house" or "because I want to have children," and not "because I want to be with you always, and to have a life that is shared." One marries because one loves that unique, irreducibly individual person, not for some purpose extrinsic to that person.

For the aesthete, love must be glamorous and look either like a conquest or a grand passion. Consider meeting a friend on the street, whom you have not seen in years. As you talk, his wife comes down the street. They greet each other enthusiastically, "Darling!" and embrace madly. They actually saw each other only an hour ago, but they greet each other as though your friend has been to war for five years and just returned.

Married love has its glamorous moments, but it is not based on glamour. It is also very ordinary and common, as is the fact that people get married every day. A marriage is a public, legal, and sometimes also a religious act, so that it is a *social* fact, with social obligations and demands that need resolution and effort in order to be met.

Should an aesthete marry, he or she will then need *externals* to keep the marriage interesting. They need things, such as a fine home and furnishings, that can be shown to other people in order to prove to others and to themselves how worthwhile it all is. For the ethical person, the outward trappings do not make the marriage and because they do not make it, they cannot break it. The excitement and the drama are not in getting and arranging externals so as to demonstrate success. Of course, it is fun to get a new house, or a piece of furniture, but the purpose of their acquisition is not to demonstrate success. The drama is the struggle and the victory of remaining sincere, patient, and loyal to the other. The success of the marriage is secured as the partners win mastery over themselves; each does it for the sake of the other. Without resolution, love ceases, both in adversity and in prosperity.

The aesthete thinks that love belongs to youth and to the vigor and beauty of youth. Marriage is merely an artifical bond once the inner vitality of youthful love has passed. Only the young can give each other "that look."

It may sound impossible, says the Judge, but love is *not* an exclusive possession of the young. Even though a person gets older and loses youthful charm, there is a beauty which love bestows to each stage of life—that of maid, bride, mother, and grandmother. For both the subject of love and the object of love change together. Married people may not give each other "that look," but this does not mean that they are not able to look lovingly at one another. That is something an aesthete cannot do.

An aesthetic marriage is always threatened by uncertainty because the marriage itself is based on uncertainties. For example, it may be based on the husband's perception, "She is the prettiest woman in town," or the wife's, "He is a man among men." But if the woman changes, or if a prettier woman comes along, or if the man ceases to be a lion, or a lion with a bigger roar comes along, then what happens? A marriage that is based on externals shares the uncertainties of externals.

The ethical person's marriage is not continually threatened with uncertainties. No merely external conditions produced the marriage in the first place, so, the Judge says, he cannot imagine any which could destroy it. If anything is certain in his own life, says the Judge, it is his marriage; for it is based on a promise, a resolve, a pledge. That promise is a fact and cannot ever cease to be a fact. Its very certainty as fact can uphold someone through all trials.

Underlying all these points of contrast is the factor with which we began, commitment. The aesthete is really afraid of commitment because it is not the *person* he loves, but rather the person specified by all kinds of externals. He loves excitement and the idea and thrill of romance. This is clear from the fact that the aesthete perceives time as an enemy; for time wears away beauty and threatens all other externals. The Judge knows how to deal with the passing of time by the secret of commitment. He must develop his character in order to keep his commitment. In this way the original datum of love is not only preserved, but with time it develops and grows. Commitment does not make life easier, but it does make it deeper. It gives it meaning and significance.

Once again let me emphasize that the Judge has not tried to prove that every marriage is happy, nor that every marriage can become happy simply by our claiming that it is permanent. But he does claim to have shown that the institution of marriage, which indeed introduces severe limitations into a person's life, does not destroy freedom. Marriage gives us the opportunity to become more fully ourselves and thus to realize one of life's great possibilities. The Judge's point of view also warmly endorses love between man and woman, but it is a romantic love stripped of the false and unrealistic ideas which surround views of love found in literature and in the popular press.

Now Kierkegaard does not endorse everything that is said by the Judge. The Judge lives in the ethical category only. The Judge does slip over into the religious domain because it is impossible to recognize marriage as an unconditional obligation without introducing a religious dimension, as we shall see. But the Judge intends to give only an ethical view of marriage. Thus Kierkegaard, writing under still another pseudonym in the *Concluding Unscientific Postscript*,[38] says that there are a few difficulties that the Judge failed to notice. In order to solve them, we must go beyond the aesthetic and ethical views of love and marriage to a religious one. Just as an ethical outlook does not reject everything that is in an aesthetic one, for it seeks to preserve and develop romantic love, so too the religious outlook does not exclude all of the aesthetic and ethical.

Marriage, religiously considered, includes a human erotic love: we do not marry just anyone, but someone whom we desire.[39] It includes a promise or vow, an unconditional obligation. But a religious person does not seek to defend the institution of marriage solely on the grounds of happiness, as does the Judge (especially in Kierkegaard's *Stages on Life's Way*). Marriage is indeed one of life's great possibilities, a possibility which may be realized, and one genuinely to be striven for. But to make the ultimate defense of marriage the possibility of happiness is a mistake.

People who are mature Christians know that the fundamental foundation of marriage is the same as the fundamental foundation of life, namely, the conviction that our goal and end is beyond every merely human state and condition. Our goal is instead the kingdom of God, which is only partly realized at present. This view gives a person enormous freedom and stability. For it recognizes that no finite creature or human institution, even one intended and endorsed by God, such as marriage, can ever give a person fulfillment. Thus a Christian does not demand more of a person than any person can give. He or she does not expect of an institution more than it can give. When each marriage partner recognizes that the beloved is also a creature, unable to satisfy all his or her needs and desires, unable to give perfect felicity, then each partner can give the other only what they are able to give. Ask too much—ask for everything—and then even that which human beings *can* give is lost.

In marriage, we indeed make a promise and undertake an obligation. A great good is possible only if we do undertake this commitment, which opens up one of life's great possibilities. But the good that then becomes possible cannot justify making an *unconditional* commitment, for our obligations continue even when the great good is not realized, and when on the basis of any reasonable calculation and expectation, it *will* not be realized. So the only possible basis for the endurance and continuation of the state of marriage is a quite "arbitrary" element, arbitrary from every human point of view, namely, a vow taken before the eternal God. From either the aesthetic or ethical point of view, a person who undertakes a pledge which binds her unconditionally is utterly arbitrary and absurd. It is for this reason that the Judge actually slipped over into the religious category. Although he can defend marriage as the friend of love, and so portray one of life's great possibilities, that possibility cannot underwrite the unconditional nature of the marriage vow. It would turn the vow into a *means* for attaining a great good; whereas the vow is unconditional.

Romantic Love and Marriage

Marriage can indeed be the friend and enhancer of love, but this good cannot be attained without an unconditional commitment. By the same reasoning, the vow is unconditional in that it is made before God. Because one's goal and end in life is the kingdom of God, one does not have to realize a profitable return in any human venture, including marriage, to obey God.

Of course this is rather offensive. But offense is one of the signs that we have indeed encountered the eternal. The offense, however, melts away before faith. For God's requirements are not arbitrary. The existence of an institution in which we may live a life together has as its intention to be constructive. It seeks to create significant lives, and it does this by giving all of us dignity. Only something which is *irrevocable* is serious. So every marriage has a seriousness, indeed, the seriousness of the presence of the holy, and gives a dignity to those who undertake to enter the state of marriage, however ordinary or humble they may be. The vow to be faithful to one another, which viewed humanly is absurd and arbitrary, and which we can find dozens and dozens of reasons to break, gives us all a dignity. We, transient beings, can perform an irrevocable act, an act which introduces eternity into time, the divine into human life.

Marriage also seeks to create people who can recognize "otherness," because it is a pledge to seek the good of the beloved. Each of us gives ourselves to the other. Whenever any condition is introduced, it indicates that however much is given, we do not give *ourselves*. The pledge is not only an act of giving, but also an act of receiving another person, of being bound to seek another's welfare. One of the wonderful things about being in love is that at first this giving and receiving is easy to do. Romantic love not only gives us the goals God has for us in our own experience—to love well, always, and faithfully, goals which can be achieved only by the guid-

84

ance and strength provided by ethical and religious commitment—but also helps us in the early stages of achieving it. What is easy and joyous introduces us to our task: to become always what we are not. We are to care for the beloved even when the task is no longer easy and effortless, even when all earthly calculations and desires tell us to flee. In this way we find neighbors in our spouses, whom we are to love as our selves, and in finding our neighbors, we find the proper way we are to love.

In his "address" at a wedding, "Love Conquers All," the document from which I have drawn much of this presentation of the religious view of marriage, Kierkegaard is very hopeful about the state of this marriage because the people being married are religious people.[40] They are committed to the kingdom of God. They are committed to love of neighbor. So they have every reason to hope that in their marriage they shall indeed achieve one of life's great possibilities. They have every reason to trust that God's love at work in them will keep their human love for each other from turning into hate, that they will be kept from destructive jealousy and possessiveness, that their love will be able to bear all things and endure all things.

Although Kierkegaard does not discuss the possibility of divorce for Christian people, I take responsibility for saying that within the Christian conception of marriage divorce is a contradiction. An irrevocable vow is just that—irrevocable. There are no rules by which we can state on what basis the marriage is dissolved. However it is also true that at every point in the course of human life and in every human venture, there is failure. The reasons and causes of failure can run the gamut from the utterly understandable to the utterly despicable. And the heart of the Gospel is that at every point and place in human life one may find divine forgiveness. Marriages will fail, just as mature Christians have failed and will fail in other endeavors. But we also know that we deal with divine love and that we can hope to be restored in ways that cannot be codified. So in the next chapter we shall state more fully the intention of marriage. We can then judge when that intention has not been achieved.

Even when the intention has not been achieved, this does not tell us that the marriage must be dissolved, or that it ought to be dissolved, or that it is in fact dissolved. It may be a basis for saying that a divorce *can* be sought because of the failure to achieve the intention of marriage. But before we turn to this, there is still another issue concerning romantic love and marriage which must be examined. Here let us only say on the issue of marriage and divorce that Kierkegaard's title in his address at a wedding was indeed well chosen, not only for marriage but for all our endeavors: "Love Conquers All."

Rather than rejecting romantic love in the name of Christian love, as does Nygren with his rejection of all human loves, I have defended romantic love by connecting it to the institution of marriage and to the recognition of "otherness," which lies at the heart of Christian love. A more realistic view of love is the result. Such realism involves the rejection of the romantic notion that there is an emotion which can take us over, which by itself and without any effort on our part can carry us to happiness with another person. Talent alone does not enable one to play tennis as a champion without resolution and practice, nor does a good voice enable one to be a concert singer without hard work. Likewise there is no emotion which by itself will enable one to live happily with another person.

Since love between people is not to be identified with a single emotion, there are feelings which, combined with traits of character such as honesty and consideration of others, enable us to love well, always, and faithfully. This love does not lead to "bliss" or to utter self-fulfillment, as is claimed in some versions of romantic love, but it does enable us to give and to receive what lies within the scope of finite creatures. We are to be stewards of these emotions. We are to act responsibly so that this gift may realize the intentions present in love. The best preparation for this task, or what comes to the same thing, the best preparation for marriage, is the same as the best preparation for life: to become a responsible person.

These are serious modifications of the popular notion of romantic love. It might even be thought that romantic love itself has been rejected here, rather than many of the ideas which have become attached to the love between man and woman. But I believe that this is not the case, for there is one feature which does not have its origin in Platonic or Christian views of love: namely, the immense *value* of an exclusive and intense attachment between a man and a woman. This must be called romantic love, and it is this which I have sought to present in a realistic way. Such a view does not do violence to Christian love, because the uniqueness of each particular love between a man and a woman is respected by Christianity's understanding of commitment in marriage. It views marriage as the institution which enables love between man and woman to achieve its ends or intentions. But Christian love itself is not an exclusive and intense attachment between a man and a woman.

Romantic love has sometimes been rejected by means of an improper use of some of Freud's ideas on the origins of love. According to Freud, all love (not just that between men and women) has its source in infant sexuality. Love

> originates in the capacity of the ego to satisfy some of its
> instincts autoerotically through the obtaining of organ

> pleasure. It is primarily narcissistic, is then transferred
> to those objects which have been incorporated in the
> ego, now much extended, and expresses the motor
> striving of the ego after those objects as sources of plea-
> sure.[41]

From this theory it is inferred that what we really and uncon-
sciously desire in romantic love is sexual release. This is thought to
cut the nerve of the romantic view, in which love is an intense and
exclusive attachment between a particular man and a particular
woman, because sexual release can be achieved with any number of
different partners.

Even should Freud himself be on the right track in tracing the
origin of all love to a desire for organ pleasure in infancy, it is il-
legitimate to identify the *present* function of love with the *origins* of
love, as has been done in the objections that are raised against romantic love. The function of various kinds of love may have different or additional meanings. We are indeed rooted in physical acts,
but our actions express meanings and intentions through physical
actions which signify more than the acts themselves. Thus romantic
love involves sexual desire and sexual expression, but what is signi-
fied in romantic love is more than sexual release.

In his influential book *Love and Will*, the psychiatrist Rollo
May raises several telling objections to some popular myths about
sex in our culture. He cites several studies to show that sex is not a
primary, all-encompassing drive even in some animals, much less in
human beings.[42] He also points out that sexual desire is not merely
the expression of a need.

> If love were merely a *need*, it would not become per-
> sonal, and will would not be involved: choices and other
> aspects of self-conscious freedom would not enter the

picture. One would just fulfill the needs. But when sexual love becomes *desire*, will is involved; one chooses the woman, is aware of the act of love, and how it gets fulfilled is a matter of increasing importance. Love and will are united as a task and an achievement. For human beings, the more powerful need is not for sex per se but for relationship, intimacy, acceptance, and affirmation.[43]

According to May, the personal aspect of love is evident in the human sexual act itself.

The fact that love is personal is shown in the love act itself. Man is the only creature who makes love *face to face*, who copulates *looking* at his partner. Yes, we can turn our heads or assume other positions for variety's sake, but these are variations on a theme—the theme of making love vis-a-vis each other. This opens the whole front of the person—the breasts, the chest, the stomach, all the parts which are most tender and most vulnerable—to the kindness or the cruelty of the partner. The man can thus see in the eyes of the woman the nuances of delight or awe, the tremulousness or the angst; it is the posture of the ultimate bearing of one's self. . . . We have to block something off, exert some effort, to make it *not* personal.[44]

Romantic love, with its exclusive attachment to a particular person, is thus not unrealistic. Even should the sexual drive in its origins be utterly plastic, so that any number of objects can give gratification, sexual desire has intimations of more than organ pleasure, though we may refuse to recognize them. Likewise romantic love has within it the intention to love another person well, always, and faithfully, though we may refuse to recognize this. Sexual love in humans is a personal act, and without distortion it can find its full expression in an exclusive attachment between a man and a woman.

Now that we have seen the connection between marriage and romantic love, and shown how marriage enables love to achieve its own ends or intentions, and have defended the "realism" of an exclusive attachment between a man and a woman, we need to consider more fully the nature of marriage itself. Only when its nature is understood is it possible to discuss the place of divorce, which has become such a serious problem in our society.

God created man in his own image,
in the image of God he created him;
male and female he created them.

Genesis 1:27

Peter Lombard observed that Eve was not taken from Adam's head, because she was not intended to be his ruler, nor from his feet either, because she was not intended to be his slave, but from his side, precisely, because she was intended to be his companion.

Eileen Power, *Medieval People*

Marriage and Divorce

As I pointed out in the last chapter, divorce is a contradiction from the Christian point of view because it is contrary to the intent of Christian marriage. But marriages quite often end in·divorce, especially today. Church people have either continued to oppose all divorce, except in cases of infidelity, or simply accepted present-day social attitudes. The trouble with going along with the views prevalent in our society is that these have seriously undermined the meaning of marriage, which becomes increasingly trivialized as divorce laws become more and more liberal. This fact has consequences for the position that does not recognize any basis for divorce beyond sexual infidelity. Often this view is held without any examination of the nature of marriage in order to determine whether divorce is indeed possible, in spite of the fact that it is contrary to the intent of marriage. We need to examine the nature of marriage to see if there is a tenable position on divorce which is neither lax nor rigid.

A Christian view of marriage is based on an understanding of people and of God's intentions for them. From this view emanates a form of marriage and a form of love which is appropriate for people, furthering and enhancing their lives. A Christian view of marriage is not determined by a commitment to maximize enjoyment, as we saw in Kierkegaard's comparison of an aesthetic and an ethical view of marriage. Once we have a Christian understanding of the nature of marriage, we can determine from its character whether divorce is ever warranted and what, if anything, may justify it. Such an approach respects the integrity of marriage; for divorce is to be sanctioned, if sanctioned at all, by reasons which are intrinsic to the nature of marriage itself.

This approach requires more of us than does either a rigid or a lax position on divorce; to use it, we must have an understanding of God's intentions for us and, specifically, his intentions for us in marriage. So even though we have already said something about marriage in the previous chapter, we must now examine its nature from the point of view of determining what may warrant the termination of a marriage.

There is today a growing discrepancy between a civil or legal view of marriage, our social and personal expectations, and a theological or Christian view of marriage. Church people are affected by all three, and everyone in our society is affected to a degree by Christian ideas which have shaped our laws and our society. We thus need to examine all three points of view and the way they affect each other.

Let us begin with our social and personal expectations. In our society today love is generally considered to be the basis of marriage. But this has not always been the case. For example, in western Europe in the sixteenth and seventeenth centuries, marriages were contracts arranged between families, at least among people of means. A person was not a solitary individual but part of an extended family, and the family's reputation and standing was very important. The continuation and enhancement of the family's name through suitable marriages was a major preoccupation. Negotiations and contracts concerning dowry and inheritance of property were conducted as serious business undertakings. A prospective bride or bridegroom had the right to veto a family's choice, but this right was often ignored.

Toward the end of the seventeenth century, and increasingly in the eighteenth, young people selected their own spouses and parents, instead of children, could veto a selection. The choice, however, was not made on the basis of being in love. Sexual attraction and romantic love were explicitly rejected as ephemeral; they were not considered a suitable basis for marriage. Rather, what was sought as a basis was "well-tried affection." This is not to say that family interests and property were not still powerful motives, but there was a perceptible shift to "well-tried affection." Marriage developed some of the characteristics found in friendship. Spouses became companions, spending more time in each other's company, apart from the rest of the extended family and in relative isolation from support and interference. This companionship was much more prevalent in Britain than in France. French visitors to Britain were amazed to find husbands accompanied to the theatre and races by their spouses; in France, husbands and wives each had their own circles of companions for these and other social occasions. Moreover, women began to play a larger role in the conduct of family affairs as they became better educated.

At the same time there was a significant change in the practice of child rearing. No longer was it thought necessary to beat children severely to overcome the effects of original sin. Kindness was thought to be more effective. With the reduction in infant mortality, moreover, people felt they were able to express more affection and become more attached to each child as a unique person. By the end of the eighteenth century, the practice of swaddling (wrapping an infant tightly to immobilize it) was abandoned and breast feeding increasingly became a mother's, rather than a wet nurse's, task. Close physical contact and care led to more affection between mother and child, and this in turn created greater intimacy between father and child as well.

The obverse side of stronger family bonding was that for the first time in western history we see the phenomenon of the spoiled child. This trend was reversed in the Victorian era, but the spoiled child reappeared in the twentieth century. It now seems that personal gratification is destroying the kind of family life which allowed it to arise in the first place. One can sympathize a little with the strictness and formality of the Victorians when one realizes how difficult it is to keep from over-indulging children. It takes the wisdom of Solomon to strike a balance between harshness and indulgence in practice. No wonder Miss Manners, who tries to do this in our day, has such a readership.

Lawrence Stone, the Princeton historian on whose authoritative work this account is based, comments that the shift in balance from family interests to well-tried affection as a basis for marriage led to more happy marriages, but to more unhappy ones as well. Adultery increased; there were more broken marriages and separations, although divorce was almost impossible in England at the time. One of the root causes may well have been the fact that with higher expectations, there was scope for more disappointment.[45]

This dynamic of higher expectations and greater disappointments is an important guide in the evaluation of attitudes toward marriage and divorce. Not only are our expectations of marriage today far higher than they were two centuries ago, but also some of our expectations actually contradict each other. There is more disappointment in marriage partly because we expect so much from it and partly because so many of us subscribe to contradictory social expectations without realizing it.

Consider, for example, our attempt to base marriage on romantic love. The eighteenth century was well aware that it is an unstable basis; we fall into love and just as easily fall out of love. Yet marriage is supposed to be permanent. Romance and permanence do not go together. In the sixteenth century John Milton, who championed the idea of romantic love in marriage, took the logical step of insisting on the necessity of divorce should such love die. Kierkegaard's attempt in the nineteenth century to combine love and marriage was indeed a very heroic effort. Unless we are prepared to love ethically, in Kierkegaard's sense of the ethical, we are trying to combine two things that do not go together. Even if we do develop Kierkegaard's realism, we must recognize that a love that grows in richness is not a certainty, but only a possibility. Otherwise we are indeed in the naive position described with admirable bluntness by de Rougemont: "Why should neurotic, selfish, immature people suddenly become angels when they fall in love and live happily ever after?"[46]

We also expect wives, and now husbands, too, to be glamorous sexual beings in both appearance and performance. This is not only because our culture so much prizes glamour and sexual pleasure, but because sex is supposed to be at the root of fulfillment. Love and sex, once thought to be the solution to life's quest, have now become one of its greatest problems. Rollo May writes,

> So great was the emphasis on love as the resolution to life's predicament that people's self-esteem ascended or fell depending on whether or not they had achieved it. Those who believed they had found it indulged in self-righteousness, . . . Those who failed to find it felt not simply bereft to a greater or lesser extent, but, on a deeper and more damaging inner level, their self-esteem was undermined. . . plagued with the gnawing conviction that they had somehow missed the great secret of life.

> In such a contradictory situation, the sexual form of love—lowest common denominator on the ladder of salvation—became our preoccupation. . . . But sex, too, has become Western man's test and burden more than his salvation.[47]

As Thomas Gould puts it, "Once war, moral ties, and temptation threatening the immortal soul were the tests of manhood; now the supreme test is the ability to satisfy a woman. It is hard to say whether homosexuality or impotence is the greater nightmare."[48]

An unrealistic view of romantic love and unrealistic sexual expectations both appear to promise a happiness in marriage that is meant to be a resolution of the human quest for salvation. We are mistaken in thinking that Christian marriage of itself can provide salvation. Furthermore, these unrealistic expectations make it impossible for the institution of marriage to provide the blessings that it *can* offer.

We expect our spouse to be a friend, indeed, to be our best friend. This may happen, but is it a requirement of marriage? In our confusion over the nature of friendship, we ask a spouse to be something we do not ask of friends. A spouse is to take an interest in everything a husband or wife does, but this contradicts the nature of friendship, which is based on freedom. As if this were not enough, parents are also required to participate in their children's interests. Then, on top of all this, marriage is supposed to allow us to realize our potential, enable us to grow, and not cut us off from any of life's interesting and desirable experiences. Is it surprising that people are disappointed with their marriages when their expectations are so demanding and contradictory?

Our expectations of family life, with or without children, also have contradictory pressures. In comparison to our very recent past, the family has lost most of its economic and educational functions. In an industrial society, which is highly mobile and competitive, the extended family has no place and the smaller nuclear family is sought as a refuge. Nicholas Lash writes, "It provides adults with an escape from the competitive pressures of the market, while at the same time it equips the young with the inner resources to master those pressures."[49] It provides a "privileged emotional climate," the prime locus of love and intimacy in our society. Yet we also resent demands and limitations placed on us by the family as a hindrance to our personal fulfillment, careers, and freedom. The drive toward personal emancipation, which is like a tidal wave washing over our century, blinds us to another value, the value of bonds which enable us to make claims and experience intimacy. In a truly intimate relationship each person may make unique claims upon the other—claims for services, affection, respect and attention—which can be supplied by that one person only. Yet the quest for personal liberation spells trouble for a permanent relationship:

> The object of emancipation is the individual, not the connection between individuals... the doctrines of this emancipation stress terms like 'self-awareness,' 'self-fulfillment,' 'self-discovery,' 'self-determination,' and 'self-sufficiency'—terms that crowd anybody other than the 'self' right out of one's imagination. The doctrine claims that the relationships between people will be better, on the whole, for the participants having been emancipated, but even if this is sometimes true, it is fairly plain that the better relationship is not the goal in itself; what is considered worth working for is the individual self-fulfillment possible within the better relationship. (When the relationship—no matter how good—gets in the way of self-fulfillment, it is clear which one has to go.)[50]

We cannot expect the family to be a haven, to provide a climate of "privileged emotion," to be truly intimate, and yet simultaneously focused on personal liberation and emancipation. Liberation and emancipation are political words, and say nothing about creating bonds. Privileged emotions do not simply arise through our wanting them, but from the claims we can make on others and the claims that can be made on us. The freedom to have this privilege—the freedom given by the kind of family that is often sought in our society today—is possible only by exorcising a contradictory understanding of freedom that regards each individual as a sovereign state, entering and exiting from relationships according to its own self-interest. This view of freedom may be legitimate in the politics between sovereign states, but it is incompatible with the desire for the intimacy of a family of two or more people.

With our extremely high expectations of marriage, as well as the contradictions inherent in some of our expectations, it is not surprising that many people's marriages disappoint them. The pressure for liberalizing the laws on divorce increased as our expectations rose and our disappointments multiplied. We often forget that there is a difference between a civil marriage and a church marriage, because the clergy are empowered to function simultaneously as an official at both kinds of marriage. There is an important conflict between civic and social attitudes towards marriage that sheds light on the tendency among church people to be either rigid or lax in their attitude toward divorce. So it is important to consider the civil attitude toward marriage.

Marriage, unlike friendship, is a public institution. Since marriages have public consequences in which the state has an interest, it regulates them by law, and so the obligations of marriage can be enforced by law. From this point of view, the family is an economic unit, with important protective and educational functions. Future members of the state are produced by married couples, who are responsible for their care and nurture. Up until recently, care and guidance were provided by the mother and the material needs by the father. (In an agrarian economy the division is less marked.)

Marriage and Divorce

The state has no particular interest in why people marry nor in their expectations. In the event of the break-up of a family by divorce, laws determine the division of the property, guarantee the continued care and nuture of children and, until recently, the economic security of the wife. The state is interested in the stability of the social order, which is not to be taken lightly—as those who have lived in a crumbling social and political situation know. The family has always been considered a necessary condition of social stability, and the permanence of marriage according to Christian teaching has suited the civil state's interests very well.

The rise in personal expectations for marriage and the contradictions in our expectations have increasingly put pressure on the state to make divorce easier and easier. In America and Britain the state, seeking to protect civic interests, resisted this pressure. In order to maintain its interests it frequently sought support from the church, calling upon it to reaffirm the permanence of marriage. But the Christian teaching that marriage is a life-long commitment was the *only* aspect of Christian teaching in which it had an interest. With the increasing social pressure for liberalization of divorce laws, the state was left with only two options: continuing to make it difficult to obtain divorce, or introducing, as many states have, divorce laws that are so liberal that they make marriage itself seem pointless. There are only two options, rigidity or laxness, because our secular understanding of marriage provides no basis for requiring it to be life-long. Without a Christian understanding of the nature of marriage, the insistence on the life-long character of marriage seems arbitrary. This is especially the case when a population is in excess of its economic or military needs, and when the bulk of educational and recreational needs of children (and in some cases nutritional needs) are provided by social institutions not dependent on a maritally-based family. In addition, from the point of view of the state, once children become independent adults, there is no need for parents to remain married.

Given the widespread ignorance of the meaning of Christian marriage among church people themselves, well-meaning people could only affirm the permanence of marriage in a legalistic way, since they could give no grounds for its continuation. For the same reason other well-meaning church people, responding to the misery in some marriages, could only drift in the direction of laxness.

One of the problems is that quite a lot of church teaching in past ages was not itself sufficiently Christian. In his exhaustive and penetrating work, *The Man-Woman Relation in Christian Thought*, D.S. Bailey argues that to a large extent the church accepted the prevailing views of marriage, sex, and the family held by first-century Judaism. The licentiousness in the ancient Roman world had led to an ascetic reaction among Hellenic philosophers. Early Christian teachers were very receptive to this asceticism, partly because Jesus himself never married and partly because they held to Paul's teachings on sex and marriage, which were heavily influenced by his expectation that this world would shortly come to an end. The celibate state was extolled as superior to that of marriage, although the latter was always said to be ordained by God and hence good. Nonetheless the ascetic fear of the sensuous led theologians to regard even marital sex as tainted with sin; the main purpose of marriage became the procreation of Christian children. The value of sex as an expression and enhancement of married love was not recognized.[51] On the contrary, marriage was seen as the remedy for the human concupiscence that was a regrettable result of the Fall, giving sexual drives a legitimate outlet.

Paul's attitude toward sexual matters, though it stops short of a dualist rejection of the body as evil, nonetheless marks marriage as a remedy for lust and exalts virginity as a religious ideal. This attitude greatly hindered a fully developed view of the goodness of marriage and of the value of love between man and woman. However much Paul sought to modify contemporary family practices by comparing the church to a bride and Christ to her bridegroom, the subordination of women to men in his injunctions on marriage allowed contemporary pagan attitudes to prevail with vastly more force than the understanding of human life unveiled by the Gospel warranted. The New Testament forcibly asserts the spiritual equality of male and female. Christ's teaching of the supreme obligation of love and forgiveness, and the power of new life that he bestowed, were not able to change the institution of marriage radically in the early centuries. Yet the influence of this understanding of human life has the potential for bearing fruit; for example, at the the time of the Reformation it helped lead to the rejection of celibacy as a state superior to marriage. Not until the present generation, however, has a distinctively Christian view of marriage begun to emerge. Only now, with the radical changes in family structure and the impossibility of seeing our society and the church as coextensive, is a distinctive theological (in contrast to civic and social) view of marriage being formulated. It has yet to be taught to very many clergy and laity. Let us now look at this emerging theological view of the nature of marriage, one largely shared by both Protestant and Roman Catholic theologians in spite of their sharp differences on birth control and abortion.[52]

Virtually all the social expectations of our society are distorted and exaggerated shadows of Christian teachings about human life and marriage. Romantic love, as we have seen in Kierkegaard, is not to be considered a rival to Christian marriage. The human aspirations for intimacy, communion, community, and freedom are all part of the very substance of life; when free of their mythical trappings, they are part of the goodness of life God intends us to enjoy. Even self-realization and self-fulfillment are echoes of God's intention that we seek and find abundant life. The expectations of Christian marriage are high, but they are also realistic because of the hope Christ's love, forgiveness, and power gives us.

The goal of Christian marriage is that "two shall become one flesh" (Mk. 10:7). This oneness is not to be limited to sexual intercourse. In this saying Jesus is alluding to Genesis 2:18-24, where it is written that "it is not good that man should be alone." None of the animals is sufficiently like Adam to provide for even the possibility of the kind of communion which would satisfy his nature. Eve is made from his very flesh. Because they are the same kind of creature, yet of different sexes, they have the basis for a communion which is satisfying. The oneness of communion in Christian marriage is not mutual absorption, so that two people become one person. Rather, their oneness is the creation and participation in a common life, which is made possible by each person sharing themselves uniquely in the state of marriage. Each is to respect the irreducible independence of the other, and to seek the other's good. The image I used earlier to express this common life is that of an elipse. An elipse is an oval figure with two foci, in contrast to a circle, which circumscribes only one point. Sexual love both expresses and enhances the spouses' common or shared life. In addition, their relation becomes an example of human community, in which the individual finds life fulfilled and completed only in sharing it in various ways with others.

Adam and Eve, male and female, are said to be made in God's image. This means that every human being has worth and value. In addition, humanity is an image of God as *sexed* humanity. Neither male nor female alone reflects the divine image; only as they are properly related to each other and to others do they participate in this image. That God seeks to restore Adam and Eve and all their progeny after the Fall, instead of abandoning them, means that every human being is an irreplaceable person. It is each one of us that God knows, and he seeks the good of each one of us. One of the places where it is to be recognized and realized in this world is in the family, whether of two or more persons, and in community. The covenant of marriage is entered with mutual respect and affection. On that basis two people commit themselves through trust in each other's cooperation toward achieving the goal of the blessings of a shared life. As that trust is progressively fulfilled, it enhances respect and affection, in turn strengthening the commitment and trust for fuller cooperation. All of this lays the basis for an intimacy which gives a sense of being at one with each other, a realization of communion. The marriage ceremony is the beginning of a life-long task of realizing this communion.

The covenant is entered into in the presence of God and a congregation. This means that there is a recognition that marriage is given to us by God as a place where our irreplaceable value may be recognized and realized, and where we in turn may do the same for another. Two people in marriage claim that blessing. Marriage is not the only way we may recognize and respect the value of others and find ourselves respected and valued. But the public nature of the ceremony of marriage—performed before a congregation— makes the ceremony a proclamation to the world. What is possible in marriage is possible in any human relationship: the recognition of the irreplaceable value of every person.

There must be above all a reliance on God's grace to fulfill the promise of the blessings of marriage. Here the image Paul has used of marriage is especially relevant. The relation of Christ to the church is compared to the relation which is to exist in marriage between husband and wife. Christ is above all faithful to his church;

he does not abandon it when it fails, but is long-suffering and for-giving. In marriage we are to persevere with fidelity and forgiveness in our quest of the goal of being fully and mutually reconciled, and fully committed to seek communion with each other.

The shared life of marriage is the environment for the procre-ation of human life. Human life is to be begotten lovingly, and nourished by those for whom the child is irreplaceable. Only in such a family life, where no one is ever unwanted, can the unique-ness of each person be recognized and cherished. In the shared life of marriage a child's identity can take root and grow, as one who can make unique claims and on whom unique claims can be made. In Christian marriage people have the opportunity to participate in God's creation of human beings, and to help bring to fruition the likeness to God we all bear, a likeness that is realized as each indi-vidual finds that life is made full and complete only by sharing it with others.

The union of Christian marriage, which I have described as a shared life, includes the children of marriage. Children are a bio-logical synthesis of their parents. The joint responsibility of parents for the nuture of children derives from their unity; it also enhances that unity as they strive together for the welfare of their children. Parents must face the question of what is worth passing on to the next generation, and so they must reach agreement on what is worthwhile, good, wise, and important. This, too, has its effect on creating the shared life of marriage.

The tendency of some parents in our society to leave all choice of "values," including religious values, up to their children is really a sign that they themselves believe in so little that they find precious that it is not worth the effort to try to pass it on. Surely parents would not withhold from their children, to whose welfare they are devoted, anything that was dear to them. Children also represent their parents' belief in a future, their willingness to continue the race in face of difficulties, suffering, and danger. The refusal to have children can be a sign of despair. An understanding of marriage as a short-term, conditional commitment is an indication that our society lacks confidence that we can deal with the future, or that it is even worth the effort to try.

The blessings for which two people are joined together in holy matrimony cannot be fully stated or even known until these blessings are realized. The nature of the shared life of marriage becomes clearer as the years pass. After nearly thirty years of marriage, I continue to be amazed as more of the nature of the estate of marriage and what is involved in a shared life is unveiled. It is impossible to anticipate fully the value of ties to relatives, to the previous generation and to the new generation, as well as what it means to be a father and a husband as the years go by and new challenges of life are encountered. Marriage is a mystery which continuously unfolds. It can be known only with the passage of time and a continuation of the effort to be faithful, long-suffering, patient, kind, forgiving, and hopeful. I do not believe its depths can be exhausted in a life-time.

But what of marriages that do not discover or realize the goodness God intends us to find? A Christian understanding of God and of people is necessary for us to deal with this question. In Christianity we are taught that God judges all our endeavors. Much of his judgment rests on the very nature God has given us, so that if we violate our nature, which includes the way we are meant to be related to each other, we find things going wrong. We do not have to wait for the consequences of our actions to work themselves out, however. We can attend to God's will as found in Scripture, prayer and meditation, public worship, and church teaching. If we are open and attentive to God's will, we can often recognize that we are not acting as we should or treating another person as we should. We can examine all our endeavors and expose our lives to God's judgment because we are sustained and upheld by his love for us and by our realization that his judgment is always a call to what is better for human life. We are aware that the perfect achievement of God's purposes for us is not possible in this life. We are to seek "to live perfectly in our imperfection," as de Rougemont puts it.[53]

The Christian goal of community in marriage is a life-long project. To live perfectly in our imperfection is faithfully to hold to that goal, even though we shall fail many times and in many ways as we strive to realize its blessings. One of the reasons it used to be very difficult to get a civil divorce lay in society's realization that when people begin to encounter difficulties in married life, they usually want to end the marriage. To prohibit divorce (or to make it very difficult) meant that people had to try harder to make their marriages work. In fact, one of the arguments for the total prohibition of divorce is based on the belief that people will make a greater effort in their marriages if they realize that there is no way out.

I think that there is a more positive reason to make divorce difficult. In Christianity we believe in the power of God to forgive us and to enable us to seek to be reconciled with one another. Our failure to live up to the intent of marriage, as well as the difficulties we encounter in marriage, are an opportunity to accept God's judgment and to be open to the love and assistance which he provides when we repent of our failures. We can move to the realization of the blessings of marriage, as is true of all our endeavors, only by facing the truth of what we are and holding in faith to what we may become with God's help.

The Eastern Orthodox and Protestant churches have always recognized sexual infidelity (and a few other offenses) as grounds for divorce. The Roman Catholic Church does not permit divorce in any circumstances, citing the passage in Mark's gospel where Jesus says that the Jewish law allows for divorce as a concession to those who suffer from "hardness of heart" (Mk. 10:5), and is not to be applied to Christ's followers. In the Middle Ages divorce came to be regarded as *impossible* because marriage was a sacrament— that is, a liturgical act that conveys a special grace and creates an ontological, indissoluble *vinculum*, or bond. The only way out of an unsatisfactory marriage was annulment. By the time of the Reformation the grounds for annulment had become extensive and, because of the highly inclusive tables of consanguinity, annulments were not difficult to obtain. The Reformers objected to the sacramental doctrine and developed instead the understanding of marriage as a covenant, which stresses the nature of the relationship in marriage rather than a metaphysical ontological bond. They also objected to the very lax regulations governing annulment. In practice the most difficult church in which to obtain a way out of marriage was not the Roman Catholic Church, in which divorce was technically impossible, but the Church of England. Because annulments had become so easy to obtain, Anglican churchmen revised the tables of affinity so as to narrow the range of prohibited marriages. At the same time, failure to draw up canons on marriage and divorce forced the ecclesiastical courts to fall back on medieval canon law, so that divorce was virtually prohibited. It was only in 1982 that the Church of England voted to change its practices and allow for divorce and remarriage.[54]

To gain some light on the difficult question of divorce it is useful to examine more closely what is meant by "infidelity." Infidelity is equated with adultery. The notion of infidelity has this narrow meaning because of the Old Testament understanding of sexual intercourse. It is based on an agricultural model: the man planted a seed in the woman's womb, which then served as a field for the seed's growth. Such a model identified the children of a marriage with the father, thus establishing a patrilinear genealogy. It also reinforced the role of the male as lord of the field, making the woman virtually his property. As a field is adulterated by foreign seeds, and thus is spoiled, so a woman who allowed her womb to become impure was considered unfaithful.[55]

There is a carry-over of this view of unfaithfulness in our society. If a married man finds it more enjoyable to be with someone other than his spouse, this is not considered adultery even if the relationship becomes passionate. As long as it stops short of copulation, the man has not been unfaithful to his marriage partner. Yet if his wife suffers from this neglect and displacement and so seeks reassurance from another, engaging in sexual activity, this is considered adultery and infidelity.

I am not trying to suggest that any significant relation with another person constitutes infidelity, but we do need to broaden our understanding of it. The marriage relation may be violated in other ways—by a severe imbalance between work and family, for example, or between hobbies and family, or by a failure to participate sufficiently in the common life of marriage and family. Neglect, lack of interest, lack of respect, lack of sympathy and support; in short, whatever contributes to the alienation of a couple from each other weakens and adulterates a marriage. Extramarital sex often has as its root the increasing alienation in a marriage. Actual sexual involvement with another by our partner can give us the occasion for self-righteousness, and hence an excuse to ignore the way we may have occasioned this form of infidelity by our own.

Infidelity is the failure to live up to the covenant. Respect, affection, trust, and cooperation are needed to move toward greater intimacy and union, toward a shared life. Difficulties with money, frustrations in various aspects of life, bad luck, human insecurity and the like all require us to make the effort to continue to show respect, affection, and trust. To the extent we fail, alienation grows. We must "divorce" ourselves from these attitudes and practices, but not divorce our spouses. We are to seek to become reconciled by seeking forgiveness and by having faith that the alienation can be overcome. We can sometimes make a significant, if not a total, break with our past. Crisis in marriage is part of the path not only to the blessings of marriage itself, but to our sanctification, as we are formed more completely into a Christian and thus realize God's intention for all of our life.

The efforts to "divorce" ourselves from those attitudes and practices which cause alienation may, however, fail. People may reach the point in which the intent of Christian marriage is utterly frustrated and can never be realized. The degree of communion that was once achieved is no longer present; it is now irretrievable. Christians in such a circumstance may seek a divorce. Even if a couple is significantly responsible for the frustration of the intent of their marriage, as Christians, they need not despair. They may repent of their failures, accept their share of blame in so far as it is possible to determine it, and seek from God the grace to lead a new life. They cannot, of course, undo all the past, nor leave it all behind. Responsibilities to children, to the extended family, and to an ex-spouse remain. But Christians are not required to continue a marriage when the intent of that marriage has been utterly frustrated. We are given the state of marriage by God for our good; when that good cannot be obtained and two people are utterly alienated from each other, then the very nature of marriage—so understood—is the grounds for divorce.

The grounds for Christian divorce differs significantly from the grounds recognized by the law, which today grants divorce for "incompatibility" and "irreconcilable differences." These terms are very loosely construed to include failure to grow, or lack of fulfillment for either spouse. But these social expectations of growth and fulfillment are not part of the nature of Christian marriage, for we are concerned instead for the good of the other, which may mean serious sacrifice in some circumstances. In addition, "incompatibility" and "lack of fulfillment" in this popular cultural sense are probably to be found to a degree in nearly every marriage. The laxness of divorce laws, the tendency to interpret them along the lines of our social expectations, is evident in many states where a mutual statement of incompatibility is sufficient justification for divorce.

But at what point does the intent of Christian marriage become utterly frustrated and without reasonable hope of being realized? Are any specific offenses, such as chronic gambling, drinking, adultery, desertion, or chronic physical abuse, grounds for a Christian to seek divorce? My intention is not to state what the law ought to be, either civil law or canon law. It is rather to give guidance to the Christian conscience, and to those pastors who are called upon for help, by describing the nature of Christian marriage. I will leave it to them to make a judgment in specific cases as to whether the intent of marriage has been utterly frustrated. I have known instances in which a Christian is married to a chronic drinker, or to someone lazy and unfaithful, and yet something of a significant relationship continued. It is not for me or anyone else to say that such a person ought to get a divorce, although I do believe that we can say that such a person *may* get a divorce as a Christian. I think that it is important, however, that specific serious and chronic offenses be listed in canon law or other church regulations on the family in order to give guidance to both lay people and pastors. It is very easy to deceive ourselves, especially when we are romantically interested or involved with another person—as is so often the case when people are having marital difficulties and considering divorce. Besides, there are always incompatibilities and even irreconcilable differences between married people; often the full promise of marriage is not achieved. A list of specific offenses can help us recognize that most of our difficulties in marriage are of the common or garden variety, and not sufficiently serious to warrant a divorce. The principle that should determine which offenses provide adequate grounds for a Christian divorce is that they cause such alienation as to prevent the intent of marriage from being realized.

Some ethicists such as Philip Turner, whose important articles on divorce I have cited in the footnotes, distinguish the issue of remarriage from that of divorce. There are good pastoral reasons for making this distinction. A marriage that has so seriously failed to achieve the intentions of marriage as to warrant a divorce is the result of serious personal failures, and not the result of mere incompatibilities or irreconcilable differences of the ordinary kind. Any divorced person ought to examine, preferably with a pastor or other spiritual guide, his or her own past with these failures in mind. It is important to minimize self-deception, as well as to gain insight into the reasons for the failure, and then to receive comfort and absolution for confession of guilt. It is necessary to wrestle with the egocentricity that lies at the root of so many of the attitudes and actions which frustrate the purposes of marriage. This not only helps us truly to "divorce" ourselves from our past, and find some degree of reconciliation with a former spouse, but it is also the only responsible way to approach the possibility of remarriage. Through such an examination, a person may find that because of certain habits, life goals, and responsibilities, remarriage is not really compatible with his or her Christian commitment.

Apart from this pastoral reason, there is no basis for permitting divorce while denying the possibility of remarriage. In fact, the only way divorce can be distinguished from separation is that in the one case remarriage is permitted and in the other case it is not. If "divorce" is allowed but remarriage is not, then such a divorce is no more than a separation. In both cases couples are no longer seeking to realize the goals of marriage, and in each case there are residual obligations from their previous endeavor. It is only when remarriage is permitted that a significant distinction between divorce and separation can be made. The question of whether an individual should remarry may be settled by self-examination with a pastor, as I have described above. It is also within the scope of this position for an individual clergyperson, after pastoral examination, to refuse to remarry a parishioner who desires it. The governing body of a church may determine the number of times remarriage is permitted, on the grounds that a significant number of past failures gives no realistic basis for hope that the intentions of marriage can ever be fulfilled. The Eastern Orthodox churches, for example, make provision for this by allowing remarriage twice, thus recognizing that some people have only a limited ability to achieve the ends of marriage.

The account of the nature of marriage which has been given in both the previous chapter and in this one has not always been the teaching of the Christian churches. It is a view that has developed over time, and particularly in recent years. We have had to learn the value of marriage. The Christian faith inherited a great deal from the ancient Judaeo-Christian world, and was not able to break radically from the views of the surrounding culture concerning women, family life, and sex. But this is part of what we mean when we say that Christianity is an historical religion. God seeks to bless us and to realize his purposes by revealing himself to people in different times and places—to people who frequently resist him and misunderstand him, and yet sometimes respond to him faithfully. The task of theology is to recognize the historical nature of our knowledge of God's intentions for us and to guide us in understanding his intentions for us in our own day. Thus I do not wish to be dogmatic in what I have said here about marriage and divorce; rather, it is offered in the hope of providing material for serious reflection to those who seek to live responsibly.

It would be eccentric for anyone to claim that he loved Zeus.
Aristotle, *Magna Moralia*, 1208b, 30

The Love of God and Our Love for God

All historians who have considered the matter agree that Jesus introduced a distinctive understanding of love. Love of neighbor and love for God are both found in the Old Testament, but it is Jesus who brought the two together and called them the two greatest commandments, summarizing all that is valid in the Old Testament Law and the teaching of the prophets. In addition, he gave a distinctive meaning to each commandment. When challenged by a Pharisee to explain the command to love our neighbor, Jesus told the story of the Good Samaritan. This parable emphasizes the universality of Jesus' teachings, in contrast to the ethnic exclusiveness of Judaism. It is a Samaritan who exhibits love of neighbor by helping an injured man, not the representatives of Judaism, a priest and a Levite, who pass him by. In Christianity, every person is a neighbor. Our love for God in Christianity includes gratitude for our creation and for God's self-disclosure to the people of the Old Testament. But Christian love for God has the additional dimension of gratitude for God's Son. He sent his only Son into the world to seek us, and allowed him to suffer the agony and humiliation of crucifixion for our sake.

In contrast to the universal benevolence of the love of neighbor, our human love for friends, spouse, and family is limited to only a few people. Since it is so, we are always vulnerable to the claim that human love and the love Christians are to have toward neighbor and God are not only different, but conflicting. In recent times Anders Nygren has been the main spokesman for this point of view. I have argued, however, that the recognition of "otherness," which lies at the core of love of neighbor, is also a necessary ingredient in friendship and marriage. The legitimate

116

claims of friends and family do limit the benevolence we can show to others. Yet the amount of benevolence we can show to others is also limited in its turn by the fact that to give of our time and resources to one person in need means that we have less time and resources available for others. So the fact that what we can do on behalf of friends and family limits what we may do for others does not in and of itself make these human loves incompatible with obedience to the two great commandments. After all, Jesus himself ministered to the people in ancient Israel, not the people of Rome or Athens, and when he was in Galilee he could not help those people who were in Jerusalem. Such limitations do not mean that he was not obedient to God.

A genuine conflict between human love and obedience to God is depicted by Milton in his epic *Paradise Lost*. There Milton contrasts God and Adam. God is self-sufficient. He needs nothing outside himself to enjoy a life that is abundantly rich and complete. This is why God alone can "love himself," that is, can find in himself everything that makes life utterly full. Adam, by contrast, is incapable of such solitude. He needs a companion with whom he can find life rich and glorious. God gives him Eve, whose beauty, love and mysterious "otherness" fill Adam with joy. Adam's life thus corresponds to God's life, but at a lower level. The joyful communion of Adam and Eve is an image of the fullness of the life that God enjoys.

When the serpent encourages Eve to eat the forbidden apple, it tells her that she will become equal with God. The goal of such fullness of life is good, but such a life cannot be grasped or seized. It is the life of God. God intends that Adam and Eve shall in time share in utter fullness of life with him by responding to his love with obedience; Eve seeks to have the divine fullness of life in a forbidden way. She believes the serpent when it tells her that the tree is

117

forbidden because God does not really want her to achieve fullness of life, does not want her to be equal with him. The great good she has already received from God—life with Adam in glorious, innocent, passionate communion—does not assure her of God's good will. Nor does it serve to assure her of a still greater life that God will bestow by sharing his life with his creatures. So she seeks to grasp for herself what she believes God wishes to withhold from her. Ironically, God has not only created her with the very hunger for fullness of life she seeks to assuage, but has also provided the way for it to be found—by obedience.

Adam's disobedience has an additional poignancy. Milton stresses the delight which communion with Eve has brought into Adam's life, including passionate, sensual delight. Adam becomes bonded to the one who gives him joy beyond any he had previously known. This joy now becomes his undoing. He is so bonded to Eve that when she disobeys God by eating the forbidden fruit, he chooses to disobey God as well rather than sever his connection to her. Fearfully and regretfully, Adam chooses to share her doom because she has become his life. The great good God has given Adam—communion with Eve—has set him at odds with the giver.[56]

Our human loves are greatly illumined by Milton's interpretation of the Genesis story. Alone, none of us is complete. The love of another person can give us a quality of life that is marvelous, and the early stages of love promise to give us utter bliss. But such love cannot give us utter fullness and completeness. To seek from a creature what can be found only from God is forbidden because the search is futile. Only God has unlimited abundance and, as I said earlier, to seek from a creature more than it can give is to lose even the good of which it is capable. Milton then portrays the increasing alienation between Adam and Eve, their anxiety over sexuality and sensual love which before their disobedience was untroubled and innocent. Romantic love and friendship, because they are great goods, can indeed keep us from believing in and seeking our ultimate good—communion with God.

This is true of all the good things God gives us, such as material abundance or intelligence. Consider, for example, George Herbert's poem, "The Pulley." It describes how at creation God generously gave us many good things, but deliberately withheld the gift of rest. After looking for satisfaction in earthly goods, we should at last out of weariness turn to him to find what we vainly have sought elsewhere.

> When God at first made man,
> Having a glass of blessings standing by;
> Let us (said he) pour on him all we can:
> Let the world's riches, which dispersed lie,
>   Contract into a span.
>
> So strength first made a way;
> Then beauty flow'd, then wisdom, honor, pleasure:
> When almost all was out, God made a stay,
> Perceiving that alone of all his treasure
>   Rest in the bottom lay.
>
> For if I should (said he)
> Bestow this jewel also on my creature,
> He would adore my gifts instead of me,
> And rest in Nature, not the God of Nature:
>   So both should losers be.
>
> Yet let him keep the rest,
> But keep them with repining restlessness:
> Let him be rich and weary, that at least,
> If goodness lead him not, yet weariness

The Love of God and Our Love for God

May toss him to my brest.[57]

We may prefer material goods, which we fear are threatened by devotion to God, and we may use our intelligence to cast doubt on his reality. This is why Jesus said that we must forsake the world. To forsake the world is not to hate it. We do not increase our love for God by rejecting what God has created for us to enjoy. But how are we to achieve a proper balance between our loves for the good things he has created for us and our love for the giver, who is so generous that he seeks to give himself to us in communion? How are we to conform our lives to God, so that we do not fail to find the utter fullness of life we hunger for?

A conflict between our human loves and our love for God may seem a purely academic question, because for so many of us need for God may not be experienced very strongly. Herbert's poem describes a restlessness many of us sometimes experience, but we probably do not recognize its source in the need for God. Our situation is different from that of Adam and Eve, who enjoy direct communion with God. For us, God is present at first only as a need, and that need is initially felt only very slightly and only occasionally in the form of restlessness. Restlessness can apparently be satisfied by so many of the good things in life, such as the pleasure of good food, company, and entertainment, continuing progress toward our career goals, and intellectual achievements. It takes time—years, in some cases—before people can recognize that however good these things are, they are not enough to give us complete satisfaction. Even then, the restlessness we experience does not identify itself to us as a need for God, and the restless craving for something that we cannot even name is not so overpowering that it opens us to a religious understanding of life. The vast emptiness at the center of our personality, which can be filled only by God's love, is experienced merely as a vague dissatisfaction, and we think that we shall find happiness when our more obvious needs and desires are satisfied by the good things life has to offer. We are so engaged in seeking to gratify them that our attention is constantly diverted from thinking about our restlessness and coming to a realization that nothing in this world can give us complete satisfaction.

It actually only takes some experience of life and some reflection on it to realize this fact. All we have to do is to remember those times when we thought that if we only had a better job, or could travel, or had a particular house, or a particular lover, or a family, and then to recall how happy we were for a while when we had gotten what we wanted—but soon found ourselves craving something else. I think most people are aware of this on occasion, but they forget about it once the mood has passed.

Without our realizing it, however, something important may happen during those moments of reflection. It is then that the need for God which nothing can satisfy is exposed, so that God's love finds an opening through which to enter us. His love is not felt or experienced because it is like a tiny seed planted in the vast emptiness of our need. It takes time to grow. As the seed grows, we begin to find ourselves responding to the stories about God in the Bible. We find ourselves gripped or engaged by some question, such as "What does it profit a person to gain the whole world and lose their own soul," or we find ourselves feeling guilty when we do certain things which previously did not bother us at all. The need for God, previously experienced only in the form of restlessness has now begun to be a *desire* for God. We find ourselves moved by the beauty of acts of mercy and more concerned with the importance of kindness. We may not realize it, but we now have in us the love of God that gives us a capacity which is beyond our inherent human capacities. It is not strong enough to drive out all of our egocentricity, but it does help us better to recognize the claims of others, and it can be cultivated so that we can become better and more mature people. In some people it grows very strong, so that they develop a very powerful passion for God and a desire to be fully possessed by him.

Restlessness is one way God's love can enter us. I mentioned earlier two other ways in which God's seed of love can take root: the story of a child watching an Advent pageant while surrounded by the love of her family, and the value of art in reminding us of traumas which help us reorder our emotional life. But however that love enters us, it needs time to grow; without it, we do not even have the potential for conflict between our love for God and our human loves. We have a need for God, but not a love for God that must be balanced with our human love for our friends and our beloved.

Where does the supposed conflict between love for God and our human loves lie? We have already seen that Christianity introduces an element of realism into romantic love. The Christian view of marriage enables our love for another person to achieve its intentions—to love well and to love always—intentions which human love is unable to achieve by its own power. We have also seen that both marriage and friendship require a recognition of "otherness" in order to prosper. That ingredient is at the core of love of neighbor. So the conflict lies not between Christian love and human loves, but between our need for God and our belief that fullness of life is to be found apart from God. Our need for God is sensed in our restlessness, but the goodness of other things keeps us hoping that we shall find fullness of life in the world.

The only other way God is present to us is in what we hear preached and taught on his behalf by various Christian churches. God is not perceptible, nor is his goodness experienced, as long as we do not come to a realization that the good things of this world are unable to satisfy us. The good that God has done and the good that God himself is, which are testified to by Christianity, do not move us. Only if the seed of his love has entered us do we find ourselves responding to this testimony. Otherwise the church's witness only makes us see that we must give up a lot of things that we find desirable, as well as do many things that are not attractive to us, such as help the needy, support the church financially, and attend worship services. There are many restrictions on the way we behave. We are to control our passions and to come to terms with our desire for prestige. In short, responding to God seems only to be tedious.

We do need to forsake the world. But forsaking it does not mean that we hate the world or do not think that it is good. On the contrary, because it is good and because we need material goods to live and some form of communion with people in order to live well, the goodness of God's creation is a barrier betwen us and God. We are distracted by our many needs and desires, as well as by the goodness of the created world, from an awareness of our need for God. But no matter how successful we are in getting what we desire, after a while we find it harder and harder to find things that are interesting to do and to possess. Boredom, instead of being something we all feel now and again, occurs more frequently and is harder to dispel. We become jaded. If we are sensible, we then begin to recognize that our aspirations are greater than this world can satisfy. This recognition may enable God's spirit of love to take root in us. At the outset we don't intend to give God's love an opening. We simply recognize that we cannot find the fullness of life we need and desire from anything that is earthly.

In time, God's love in us begins to grow. We experience it in the form of greater interest in things we hear or read about God, and in finding ourselves beginning to experience a conflict between our way of life and Christian ideals. If the spirit of love is not driven out in this struggle, or choked by our unchecked appetites, we find ourselves responding more positively to Christian teachings. They seems less restrictive, for we find that what we have to give up is either detrimental to a better relation with others or else opens us to something we now value. We look upon material goods, ambition, and prestige differently. Our responsibility to others is seen less as a burden and more as an opportunity.

We will certainly say things and do things which seem to deny the value of human love, especially those in whom God's love is not at work. Because nothing finite can satisfy our need for God, the love of God will be seen to be the primary task for human beings and the love of neighbor the primary way we are to be related to other human beings. We cannot say that either the love between men and women or the love between friends is more important than our love for God or our love for our neighbor. We know that our life is less rich without them, but we also know that neither of them can be proper human loves without an ingredient that is not human: namely, a recognition of the "otherness" of things. This recognition is possible because of a divine love at work in us, whether people recognize it as divine or not. However glorious our human loves may be, furthermore, we know that they do not last forever. We aspire to be with those we love forever. Divine love has no end. Its presence enables us to believe the promise of God in Christ's resurrection: because we are bonded to him with holy love, the life of God present in us now will have no end. We shall continue to share that life, and share it even more fully after we pass out of this world. At least we can come to have that conviction as we follow Christ's way and allow the seed of love to grow larger, becoming the substance of our lives.

Some people may have the vocation to renounce not only particular occupations, but also friendship, marriage, and family life. They may have tasks to do which make these things a hindrance, or even impossible. They may have this vocation simply in order to be a witness to the fact that human beings have a need for God, and that some people can have such a love for God and joy in him that they can make such a renunciation. But the fact that some people are called to express their devotion to God as a missionary, minister, priest, or member of a religious community does not imply that secular occupations are inferior to these callings, nor that friendship, marriage and family life are not desirable. Quite the contrary, it is recognized that a great deal is lost by those who renounce them. Even St. Paul, often cited as one who denigrated marriage, pointed out that unlike Peter—who was accompanied by his wife—he and Barnabas were unmarried and this was a sacrifice for them. It is only one who does not know the love of God nor have any love for God who finds the sacrifice of anything desirable appalling.

Granted that we do not respond to claims made about God at all unless we have in one way or another received the spirit of God's love, what is it about God that is so lovable? His spirit at work in us gives us the *capacity* to love him, but *why* should we love him? "We love, because he first loved us" (I John 4:19). We do not normally find ourselves under any obligation to love other people just because they love us; what this text means is that God has made the first move. It is not as though we have come to love someone who is unaware of us, simply because we find that person so marvelous. Instead it is we who are unaware of God, who loves us and has created us and given us all a great destiny. What then is that destiny?

The Love of God and Our Love for God

The most common perception of Christians is that God wants to give us life after death in heaven. Doctrinal teachings of the various churches differ over precisely what is required of us to receive eternal life, but they all teach that if we do not receive eternal life we are condemned to hell for our disobedience. I do not want to discuss here the issue of whether or not there is a hell, or what its nature is. Rather, I only wish to point out that if our sole relationship to God is to a judge who sends us to heaven or hell on the basis of whether we obey him or not, then we have not found any reason to love him. Only if victory over death and eternal life is available to us because of God's *mercy*, do we have some reason to love him.

This raises the question of how he has made it possible for us to go to heaven. Generally it is said that we all deserve to go to hell because of our sin, but that God in his mercy sent his Son into the world to suffer and die on a cross in our place. God the Father punishes him instead of us. We can indeed be grateful for our escape from the consequences of our sin, but then it is hard for us to find lovable a God who would punish an innocent person. Not only does the action seem unjust, but why, we ask, does he have to punish anybody? Can he not simply forgive us?

To answer this question, we need to look at Jesus' teachings on forgiveness. Peter once asked Jesus, "Lord, how often shall my brother sin against me, and I forgive him? As many as seven times?" Jesus answered him, "I do not say to you seven times, but seventy times seven" (Mt. 18:21-22).

Jesus introduced kindness and mercy into the world in a new way. There were many teachings about kindness and mercy in the Old Testament, but what Jesus had to say was different. This is why Peter asked him his question. The rabbis apparently taught that we were to forgive a person three times. Seven is more than twice as much as three, so Peter apparently recognized that Jesus' way was much more demanding than anything that had been taught before—more than twice as demanding. Even so, Peter had not understood the full magnificence of what Jesus taught; Jesus took Peter's seven and said to him, "Not seven, but seventy times seven."

Now, we can do our arithmetic and figure out that seventy times seven is four hundred and ninety-seven. Or we can use our heads and realize that Jesus has moved us into a completely new world. We are no longer in a world that keeps count, a world in which the issue is not three, seven, or seventy times seven. We have moved into the kingdom of his Father. There is a difference between an *act* of forgiveness and a forgiving *person*. Jesus teaches us to become forgiving people, not to ask about how many times we are to perform acts of forgiveness. It is the kind of people that we are to become that is the issue, because the kingdom of God consists of people: people who are kind, people who are merciful, people who forgive. It is not a kingdom in which the number of deeds is marked down so that with the right statistics, we are members of an elite group bound for an eternal kingdom.

That was indeed the kind of person Jesus was: merciful and forgiving. Peter, living with him, came to realize that something new and glorious had come into the world. He began to find himself moved to become a generous person because of Christ. His heart began to open, and so he found himself leaping far beyond the rabbi's teaching, more than twice as far. Jesus lifted him even further. In fact, he lifted him to another plane entirely by showing him the real question: what are we to become? He showed Peter that we are to become what he is, a forgiving person. In Christianity, it is not a legal requirement that must be met. We are to be people who live under the rule of a generous heavenly father and who belong to his kingdom. Such people are generous people, kind people, merciful people, forgiving people.

Jesus then told Peter and the others a parable, in order to make himself as clear as possible. The parable is about a man who owed his king an immense sum of money and who could not repay his debts. At first the servant was threatened with very severe punishment. But when the man begged for more time to repay, the king was so moved that he forgave him the entire debt. The king gave far more than he had been asked for (Mt. 18:23-35).

But Jesus goes on to say that this very same man, who had been so generously forgiven, turned around and demanded payment of a very small sum from another person. He did not show any mercy at all. He would not even give his debtor more time to repay, as he begged, much less forgive him the debt. When the king learned of this, he was extremely angry. He had the first man arrested and cast into prison, where he was to stay until he should pay his entire debt.

This seems fair enough, ethically speaking. After all, the unjust man deserved to go to prison in the first place because of his debt, and he deserved it all the more because of his lack of mercy. Still, the story is confusing. The king did not forgive the servant three times, much less seven or seventy times seven. He forgave him only once, and then when he failed to forgive another person, he had his servant cast into prison. Why was the man not forgiven again? How is this story consistent with Jesus' other teaching?

The parable teaches us that it is not easy to *be forgiven*. We are all prepared to believe that it is difficult to forgive, immensely difficult. Think how awful it would be if someone were spreading lies about you at your place of work. Think how serious it would be if other people, including your boss, believed what was said about you. Even so, that is not nearly as serious as the pain and injury we can receive from people who are nearest to us, people who are our friends or members of our own family. We know only too well how difficult it is to forgive those injuries. It thus seems perverse to claim that it is immensely difficult to *be forgiven*. What could be easier? Yet we learn from Jesus' parable that the difficulty is real.

The man who owed a great debt to his king never did receive the forgiveness he was offered. If he had truly received it, he would have been able to forgive as well. To be forgiven is to be changed. If he had received the forgiveness offered, he would have become a better person, a more generous person. Instead, he was the same person after he had been forgiven as he was before. The steward had not been affected in the least by his lord's mercy. Thus his debt was still outstanding. It remained in force and would continue to remain in force until it was paid.

Yet how can such a debt be paid? How can that immense load be lifted? It can be lifted in one way only: by *receiving* forgiveness, by *receiving* mercy. To receive is not easy, because to receive is to be changed. The man in the parable did not want to be changed. He just wanted to be let off an obligation, and so he suffered the consequences. God wants us to become people who live in his kingdom, and that means to become a different kind of person. This man refused to be changed. Then he had to bear his own burden, because he would not allow a generous lord to bear it.

Why is it hard to be forgiven? One reason is that forgiveness requires us to see its great cost. The king who forgave the man his debts actually suffered a great loss; the man owed him an immense sum. But the servant whom the king forgave did not notice. He was so full of his own concerns that he did not see the king as a person with feelings, too. He did not see that the king would have to make a great sacrifice so that his steward could be relieved of a great burden.

No wonder the king in the story was angry when his servant did not forgive another man's debt. This ungenerous man could not bear the pain of the loss of a few dollars even though he himself had caused his king an immense loss. He had taken the king's pain and loss for granted. To receive forgiveness is to recognize the pain and loss that a person who forgives you has to bear, to see the grief we have caused. That recognition fills a person with gratitude. Gratitude enables a person to bear pain and loss for another person's sake. But the steward was not capable of receiving. Rather, he had tried to *take* something, namely, to take his forgiveness for granted. But God does not allow us to take anything. He allows us only to receive. We cannot take anything for granted; for whatever we take will at the last return to him. This is why Jesus once said, "He who seeks to save his life will lose it."

According to this story there is no question about God's generosity. He desires that we all shall turn to him and live now and always with his spirit of love within us. But God can only enter a willing heart, a heart that wants to be changed.

So often people say: I have never experienced God. I have never felt his kindness or mercy or forgiveness. The question is, have we ever wanted to be merciful, kind, forgiving? Not once or twice or three times, not seventy times seven, but always? Have we wanted to become kind, merciful, forgiving people? The question is not the generosity of God but rather what we want to become. This is one of the reasons why God cannot "just forgive" us.

Granted that forgiveness involves suffering on the part of the one who forgives, why does not God himself suffer rather than his Son's suffering on the cross? I believe that we can get some illumination on this point from Dostoevsky's novel, *Crime and Punishment*. In this novel a young man named Raskolnikov kills a harmless old woman. He kills her ostensibly to rob her of a few coins, but in fact he wishes to assert his superiority over the conventions of right and wrong. Raskolnikov transgresses a forbidden boundary by killing a person to prove his thoughts in action. He thus seeks to assert that he is a superior person, standing on a height above others, with nothing on his horizon to limit or restrict him. Then he comes to bear the consequences of his outlook and crime, for Raskolnikov is indeed alone and must live out of his own resources without replenishment or affirmation through contact with anyone. God, in contrast to us, can dwell alone on high, above all creation, because he has the resources within himself to live. But we do not. Raskolnikov begins to feel the agony of being unable to be close to anyone, and to realize that by his transgression he is now permanently cut off. He has done something that cannot be undone. God has been perfectly just. He has given the young man what he wanted: to be alone.

There is one exception. A woman named Sonya, a prostitute who is forced to live as she does in order to help her destitute family, is the only person who can penetrate his utter isolation. Her love enables him to accept his punishment from the court as just, and together they go into exile. Raskolnikov explains why she was able to penetrate his isolation: Sonya had told him that she too had killed, but what she had killed was not another person, but herself. She had sacrificed herself for her family. Because she had "killed," Sonya was able to lead Raskolnikov to redemption from his crime and utter isolation. We have here the paradox of a criminal, one who has killed, bonded to one who is a victim, one who has been killed. The guilty and defiled thus has a tie with the innocent and pure.[58]

Dostoevsky gives us an insight into God's way of redeeming us through the sacrifice of his Son. It is not enough for the Father who loves us to suffer on account of our deeds, which injure both others and ourselves. God loves us so as to redeem us. He does not redeem us by staying at a distance, but becomes a human being in order to suffer as we suffer, and to bear what we cannot bear. He goes as far as we have strayed and transgressed. Jesus becomes an outcast of society so that outcasts may have a bond with him, and through him with his Father. He is condemned as a criminal and dies among thieves; he is a victim so he can be bonded to those who are victims; he is forsaken by all his friends and companions to be with those who are alone; he becomes utterly helpless to be with those who have no help.

Innocence and purity are bonded to guilt and defilement by a love that does not seek to impose its own way, but follows us who have departed from the way, so that no one can say, "God is not in this place; I am forsaken; there is no help for me." Jesus suffers not so that we might avoid suffering, but that our suffering may be like his. He makes our suffering like his own by becoming a human being. Jesus suffers on account of us and with us, so that the Father's arms may embrace his creatures through and in the arms of one born of a creature, his beloved Son. God is lovable because he seeks to give himself to us and to bind us to himself by becoming incarnate, and suffering.

There is one feature of the sacrifice—God's way of winning our hearts—which deserves special attention. The spectacle that the crucifixion presents is that of God, who is almighty, once again allowing creatures to use their power to resist the good he would bestow. This feature is particularly well portrayed by George Herbert in his poem, *The Sacrifice*.

> The Princes of my people make a head
> Against their Maker: they do wish me dead,
> Who cannot wish, except I give them bread:

The Love of God and Our Love for God

Was ever grief like mine?

Without me each one, who doth now me brave,
   Had to this day an Egyptian slave.
They use that power against me, which I gave:
    Was ever grief like mine?

God's response to our resistance is to endure it. He hopes to win us through our perception of his grief.

I answer nothing, but with patience prove
If stony hearts will melt with gentle love.
But who does hawk at eagles with a dove?
    Was ever grief like mine?

Herbert's point in *The Sacrifice* is that we cannot ultimately defeat God's love and design. He describes the benefits God seeks to confer on us and our blindness to this generosity, yet still God seeks us by finally coming to us in the person of Christ. The response to Christ is rejection. However Herbert shows that this cannot defeat his love. Our very hateful rejection is turned into a sacrifice. That is, instead of rejecting us for rejecting him, God takes our very rejection and turns it into a revelation. It reveals the magnitude of his love and his willingness to put up with our blindness, our folly, our evil. His response to all that we are and have done is not rejection, but painful endurance ("I, who am Truth, turn into truth their deeds"). Not only does God let us see the effects of all that we are and do by letting these "deeds" destroy his body, but he also shows us that all that we are and do will not stop him. His love cannot be turned away. Even when people killed the one who bore the love of God, God raised him from the dead to confront us once again and to claim us. Thus the greatest rejection of all still cannot defeat his love, and we are to see in the suffering our rejection causes, a precise measure and revelation of the extent and tenacity of his love.

From my personal experience I believe Herbert is correct: such love does melt stony hearts. For example, I can be in the company of people who are much more clever or accomplished than I. They do not make me feel ashamed, because I have learned that I do not have to possess enormous intellect to be comfortable with myself. I am not ashamed to be in the presence of great wealth, either, because I have learned that fullness of life is not to be found through great possessions. People who have power over me can make me afraid, but they do not make me feel ashamed because I know that the unjust use of power is immoral. Yet if someone is able to portray Christ, as the Gospel writers as well as many preachers, writers, and poets such as Herbert do, then I do feel ashamed of myself. I find that the Christ so portrayed judges my life, making me aware of its invalidity and of my inability to trust in myself.

God in all his dealings with us seeks to make us aware that we are dependent on him. He does this not in order to lord it over us, or to gratify his vanity, as is so often the case with human beings, but in order to give us the communion with him that we need but vainly seek elsewhere. This, too, is beautifully expressed in Herbert's poem, "Love III."

> Love bade me welcome: yet my soul drew back,
>   Guilty of dust and sin.
> But quick-ey'd Love, observing me grow slack
>   From my first entrance in,
> Drew nearer to me, sweetly questioning,
>   If I lack'd anything.

A guest, I answer'd, worthy to be here:
    Love said, You shall be he.
I the unkind, ungrateful? Ah my dear,
    I cannot look on thee.
Love took my hand, and smiling did reply,
    Who made the eyes but I?

Truth Lord, but I have marr'd them: let my shame
    Go where it doth deserve.
And know you not, says Love, who bore the blame?
    My dear, then I will serve.
You must sit down, says Love, and taste my meat:
    So I did sit and eat.

Although we are caught in the power both of death (the natural end of everything made from dust) and damnation (the just end of sin) neither is to be our end. Love sacrifices itself in order to relieve us of both death and sin. What can we render back for such a sacrifice? In and of ourselves we cannot even serve him; all we can do is to receive his sacrifice. We receive Christ as an act of obedience; we do not presume to take the food from the table, even though we know that our salvation from death and damnation is Christ's sacrifice. It is because Christ commands it that we sit and eat. Simone Weil also expresses this attitude in her "Spiritual Autobiography": "If I had my eternal salvation placed in front of me on this table, and if I only had to stretch out my hand to take it, I would not put out my hand so long as I have not received the order to do so."[59]

There is a certain robust simplicity in the obedience that Herbert expresses in the last line of his poem—"So I did sit and eat." After the intensity of the previous lines, the guest in effect says, "All right, you tell me to sit down and eat, so I will do as I am told!" There is a tone even of light-heartedness; indeed there should be, as the poem is an allusion to the final banquet in heaven where, we are told, there is much rejoicing.

* * *

There are at least four major views of love in western culture: Christian, Platonic, Romantic, and Freudian. Platonism was harmonized with Christianity wherever possible and thus became a part of the Christian tradition, especially in the Eastern Orthodox, Roman Catholic, and Anglican communions. Plato's stress on the Good, which exists beyond the sensible world and yet is the source of all the good of this world and can be reached by love, was easily blended with Christianity. There are clear differences of emphasis and even points of incompatibility between Christianity and Platonism, but the two are not utterly incompatible.

The only significant aspect of Plato's view of love that survives in a form independent of Christianity today is the love of theoretical knowledge. The passionate search for and joy in knowledge for its own sake is the trademark of Platonic love, and it is a pleasure for a teacher to find pupils, even children, responding with excitement and wonder to principles that give insight into the workings of our world. That sense of joy was integrated into Christianity in its speculative, mystical, and practical theology very early on. The joy with which the intellect pursues and finds truth, and our hearts discover what is worthwhile, flourishes in a very congenial environment within the Christian vision of God. God made us to enjoy the creation and to see that joy reach its culmination and consummation in a knowledge of the source of all truth and goodness.

I have said little about Platonic love in this book because it is not nearly as significant for the love between man and woman as is the ideology of romantic love. Its connections to the literary conceit of courtly love is not altogether clear, but courtly love did help create an interest in tales of romantic love and so made love between man and woman the dominant theme in western literature. Christianity is not responsible for the dominance of romantic love in our lives today, yet theologians have rendered it an important service by harmonizing its ideas with those of Christianity, as we have seen from our study of Kierkegaard's views on marriage, and thus made it a more realistic understanding of love.

"Love of humanity" or *philanthropos*, as love of neighbor is frequently called in the early church and in Eastern Orthodoxy today, is above all a Christian achievement. The absolute value of all people, as well as our obligation to help them, has its roots in Judaism but is brought to fruition by the life and teachings of Jesus. It is not the same kind of love as friendship, but friendship can only prosper and become what it intends by having love of neighbor as an ingredient.

Freudian psychology has had multiple effects on our culture and on Christianity, both indirectly and directly. Freud's own views on love developed over a period of time and often changed radically. In general we can say that one important effect of his viewpoint is to help us overcome an ascetic rejection of the body and realise more fully its more positive valuation in much of the Old and New Testament. Very early on in Christian history this regard for physical blessings was totally undermined by the influence of Hellenic asceticism. Now we regard our sexuality as part of our identity—although the cause of much distress and temptation, it is nonetheless a source of joy and blessing as well. After all, our intellectual powers have been at least as great a source of confusion and prideful rejection of God as has our sexuality, and yet it is our intellect which has most frequently been cited as bearing the image of God. We would do well, as I suggested earlier, to recognize that our own sexuality is included in what we bear as the image of God: "So God created man in his own image; in the image of God he created him; male and female he created them" (Gen. 1:27).

Christianity is the only cultural force that has made a place for all the major theories on love in western culture. It has modified them with its own distinctive understanding of love, and in turn has been modified—yet without losing its distinctiveness.The vision of Christian love is not eclectic, but has achieved a creative fusion because of its own independent vitality through the ages. Christian love has never lost sight of God as the creative source of all that has life, and as the suffering redeemer who is ever present by the power of the Spirit to those who open their hearts to his love.

Notes

1. "Love as Perception of Meaning" in *Religion and Understanding*, ed. D.Z. Phillips (New York: Macmillan, 1967), p. 151.

2. *Ibid.*, pp. 149-50.

3. Basil Mitchell, *Ethics* (Oxford: Oxford University Press, 1980), esp. ch. 9.

4. As found in Urban T. Holmes, *A History of Christian Spirituality* (New York: Seabury Press, 1981), p. 153.

5. Published by permission of Lisa Corum.

6. This understanding of art is taken from an unpublished statement written by Douglas Kinsey, Professor of Art, University of Notre Dame, for a series of nineteen of his monotypes entitled "After the Fall." I have paraphrased his remarks. Kinsey's series of monotypes was reproduced as a portfolio insert in *Boundary 2: A Journal of Postmodern Literature*, vol. 12, no. 1, Fall 1983.

7. *Nicomachean Ethics*, 1171b, 29-37 to 1172a, 1-8 in the international pagination found in the margin of most editions of Aristotle's works.

8. In his classic discussion of the basis and nature of friendship Aristotle entirely ignores sexual activity, even though he is

well aware of homosexuality in his society. C.S. Lewis carefully distinguishes friendship from erotic interest and activity. See *The Four Loves* (New York: Harcourt Brace & Jovanovich, 1960), pp. 90-93.

9. L. Rangell, "On Friendship," *Journal of the American Psychoanalytic Association*, vol. 11, 1963, pp. 3-54.

   For convenience, my entire chapter on friendship is written as if friendship were between two people only, even though it can occur between more than two.

10. *Nicomachean Ethics*, 1156a, 5-25.

11. William K. Rawlins, "Openness as Problematic in Ongoing Friendships: Two Conversational Dilemmas," *Communication Monographs*, vol. 50 (March, 1983), pp. 1-13.

12. William K. Rawlins, "Negotiating Friendship: the Dialectic of Conjunctive Freedoms," *Human Communication Research*, vol.9, no. 3 (Spring, 1983), pp. 255-66.

13. *The Four Loves*, pp. 95-6.

14. *Nicomachean Ethics*, Books 8, 9.

15. It has been assumed that the greatest friendships are those among men, but there is significant empirical evidence that men today are singularly lacking in the requisites for friendship. See William K. Rawlins, "Cross-Sex Friendship and the Communicative Management of Sex-Role Expectations,"

Communication Quarterly, vol. 30, no. 4 (Fall, 1982), pp. 343-352, and Jerome Tognoli, "Male Friendship and Intimacy Across the Life Span," *Family Relations*, vol. 29 (July, 1980), pp. 273-9.

16. Rawlins, "Cross-Sex Friendship," pp. 346-7.

17. *Love in the Western World*, rev. ed (New York: Harper & Row, 1956), p. 313.
     As we shall see in the next chapter, it is important to distinguish between the theory of romantic love and romantic love itself.

18. Rawlins, "Cross-Sex Friendship," p. 347.

19. *The Autobiography of Bertrand Russell*, 1872-1914 (Boston: Little, Brown, 1967), pp. 226-7.

20. Henri I. Marrou, *A History of Education in Antiquity*, trans. George Lamb (New York: Sheed & Ward, 1956), ch. 3.
     "The very vocabulary of the Greek language and the laws of most city-states show that homosexuality was always regarded as something 'abnormal'" (p. 26).

21. In the international pagination used in most editions of Plato, 180c-185e.

22. Marvin K. Opler, "Anthropological and Cross-Cultural Aspects of Homosexuality" in *Sexual Inversion* (New York: Basic Books, 1965), p. 114.

Footnotes

23. The United Church of Christ, *Human Sexuality: A Preliminary Study* (New York: United Church Press, 1977), p. 187.

24. Don S. Browning, *Religious Ethics and Pastoral Care* (Philadelphia: Fortress Press, 1983), pp.89-90.

25. *Ibid.*, pp. 90-91.

26. *Ibid.*, pp. 92-93.

27. Nygren mistakenly conflates love of neighbor and *koinonia*:
    "[Love of neighbor] loses something of its original, all-embracing scope; it becomes love for those who bear the Christian name. When love is said to be the evidence for those that will convince the world that the disciples of Jesus really are His, it is the love they show to each other as Christians that is meant (John 13:35), not the love that directs itself to those outside. *This clearly means that neighbourly love has lost something of the meaning it had in the Synoptic Gospels* [my emphasis]." Anders Nygren, *Agape and Eros*, trans. Philip S. Watson (London: S.P.C.K., 1957), p. 154.

28. Translation from the *New English Bible*.

29. Thomas Gould, *Platonic Love* (New York: The Free Press, 1963), pp. 11-12.

30. *Ibid.*, p. 12.

31. Virginia Woolf, *To the Lighthouse* (New York: Harcourt, 1955), p. 157.

32. See John C. Moore's review of Singer's first volume for a careful exposure of a crucial confusion in Singer's thesis that allows him to make such a charge against Christianity: "The Origins of Western Ideas: Irving Singer's *The Nature of Love: Plato to Luther*," *Journal of the History of Ideas*, vol. 29 (1968), pp. 141-51. See especially pp. 142-6.

    For an account of the compatibility of Christian love ("agape") with the human love between people, see my *Finding Our Father* (Atlanta: John Knox Press, 1974) and *Three Outsiders: Pascal, Kierkegaard, and Simone Weil* (Cambridge, MA.: Cowley Publications, 1983).

33. Most readers will probably find the abridged version of the essay sufficient for their purposes. See *A Kierkegaard Anthology* (ed.) Robert Bretall (Princeton: Princeton University Press, 1946), pp. 80-97.

34. Iris Murdoch, *An Unofficial Rose* (New York: Viking Press, 1962).

35. "The Talk of the Town," *The New Yorker*, August 30, 1976, p. 21.

36. Moore, p. 145.

37. As found in Kathleen E. Morgan, *Christian Themes and Contemporary Poetry* (London: S.C.M. Press, 1965), p. 68.

38. *Concluding Unscientific Postscript*, trans. David F. Swenson and Walter Lowrie (Princeton: Princeton University Press, 1941), p. 161.

39. Nygren denies all connection between human love and Christian love. Yet love does exist between human beings; in our society, it is considered a necessary condition for marriage under most circumstances. Thus it needs to be related properly to Christian love, especially in showing how Christian love in marriage can enable the love between man and woman to achieve its own ends, as well as how love in marriage is of value for the development of a Christian person.

    My views in what follows are partly drawn from de Rougemont, who took it from Kierkegaard. De Rougemont has been wrongly bracketed with Nygren as making human love (specifically romantic love) utterly incompatible with "agape" or Christian love, as John Moore points out in the review cited above. De Rougemont has a chapter entitled "Eros Rescued by Agape." In the name of Christian love, he rejects the idea of love as a passion connected with death. He wishes to free us from various ideas about romantic love as it has evolved from its roots in medieval courtly love, so that the love between men and women can assume human proportions. This uncontaminated human love—with the help of Christian agape—can achieve its intrinsic aim.

40. See *Thoughts on Critical Situations in Human Life*, trans. David F. Swenson (Minneapolis: Augsburg, 1941).

41. Cited in Gould, p. 13.

42. Rollo May, *Love and Will* (New York: W.W. Norton, 1969), p. 310.

43. *Ibid.*, pp. 310-11.

44. *Ibid.*, pp. 311-12.

45. Lawrence Stone,*The Family, Sex and Mariage in England 1500-1800*, abridged edition (New York: Harper & Row, 1979). I have relied primarily on Stone's public lecture delivered at the University of Notre Dame, South Bend, Indiana in the fall of 1980.

46. De Rougemont, p. 300.

47. Rollo May, *Love and Will*, p.14.

48. Gould, p. 12.

49. As found in Stanley Hauerwas, "The Moral Meaning of the Family," *Commonweal* (August 1, 1980), p.433.

50. *The New Yorker*, p. 21-22.

51. D.S. Bailey, *The Man-Woman Relation in Christian Thought*, (London: Longmans, Green, 1959). Bailey's remark about one aspect of Paul's view of sex shows that Paul was not as one-sided as is often thought today. "If there is any element of real novelty in the specific teaching of the New Testament on sexual relations, it is perhaps to be found chiefly in St.

Paul's profound and realistic treatment of coitus and its significance in the first epistle to the Corinthians. Here his
thought owes nothing to any antecedent notions, and dis-
plays a psychological insight into human sexuality which is
altogether exceptional by first-century standards. The apostle denies that coitus is, as the Corinthians would have it,

merely a detached and (as it were) peripheral venereal function involving no more than an appropriate exercise of the
genital organs. On the contrary, he insists that it is an act
which, by reason of its very nature, engages and expresses
the whole personality in such a way as to constitute an
unique mode of self-disclosure and self-commitment. It is
curious that this remarkable and pregnant concept should
have had a negligible influence upon Christian thought—
probably because it invests coitus with a significance which
proved unacceptable in the face of rapidly developing asceti-
cal tendencies in the Church." (pp. 9-10)

52. Pope John Paul II in his teachings on marriage has accepted
romantic love and the goodness of sex, intimacy and mutual
society as ends in marriage without subordinating them to
other ends, such as the perpetuation of the human race, as
has commonly been the case in most of Christian history.
See Richard M. Hogan and John M. LeVoir, *The Covenant
of Love: Pope John Paul II on Sexuality, Marriage, and Family
in the Modern World* (Garden City, NY: Doubleday, 1985).

For a sensitive treatment of married love and the family
by a Roman Catholic theologian in line with the above mentioned work by John Paul II, see William E. May, "The
Christian Family in Today's World," *Faith and Reason*, vol.
9, no. 4 (Winter, 1983), pp. 267-81.

I do not believe that the statements on divorce and abortion in either of these works, however, follow from their views of love, sex, and marriage.

53. De Rougemont, p. 302.

54. See Philip Turner, "The Marriage Canons of the Episcopal Church: (I) Scripture and Tradition," *Anglican Theological Review*, vol. LXV, no. 4 (October 1983), pp. 371-93. His sequel is also highly recommended: "The Marriage Canons of the Episcopal Church: (II) The Case from Reason," *Anglican Theological Review*, vol. LXVI, no. 1 (January 1984), pp. 1-22. For a sensitive discussion of remarriage see his sermon, "Divorce and Remarriage," in *Love and the Single Christian* (Cambridge, MA.: Cowley Publications, 1983).

55. Thomas M. Olshewsky, "A Christian Understanding of Divorce," *Journal of Religious Ethics*, vol. 7/1 (Spring, 1979), p. 122. This article has deeply influenced my thinking, especially on the nature of infidelity.

56. This interpretation of Milton was suggested to me by Irving Singer, *The Nature of Love: Courtly and Romantic* (Chicago: University of Chicago Press, 1984), pp. 241-56.

57. All quotations from Herbert's poetry are taken from *George Herbert: The Country Parson, The Temple*, Classics of Western Spirituality, ed. John N. Walls (New York: Paulist Press, 1981).

Footnotes

George Herbert (1593-1633) was a highly polished courtier with the extensive learning of a Renaissance gentleman, the Public Orator for Cambridge University, and twice a member of Parliament, in turbulent times. In 1630 he was ordained a priest of the Church of England and served the parish of Bemerton, Wiltshire until his death.

His understanding of the Christian life is to be found primarily in his masterpiece, *The Temple*, which consists of 164 individual poems. Each poem has self-contained meaning and can be read apart from the others, but they are arranged in an order that traces the Christian pilgrimage. For a description of it, see my article "The Christian Pilgrimage in George Herbert's *The Temple," Anglican Theological Review*, vol. LXVII, no. 4 (October 1985), pp. 329-47.

58. This was pointed out to me by my son, Timothy G. Allen.

59. Simone Weil, *Waiting for God* (New York: Harper & Row), 1973, pp. 24-5.